God and
Government

God and Government

The Separation of Church and State

Ann E. Weiss

Houghton Mifflin Company   Boston

Library of Congress Cataloging in Publication Data

Weiss, Ann E., 1943–
    God and government.
    Bibliography: p.
    Includes index.
    Summary: Analyzes church-state relations,
considering situations in which government and
religion have supported each other as well as
those in which the two are in conflict.
        1. Church and state—United States—Juvenile
literature.   [1. Church and state]   I. Title.
BR516.W434   322'.1'0973   81-17861
ISBN 0-395-32085-2   AACR2

Printed in the United States of America

HC ISBN 0-395-32085-2
PB ISBN 0-395-54977-9

AGM 10 9 8 7 6 5 4 3 2 1

For Kenyon and Kathie,
who have done so much

Contents

Preface

The United States Constitution provides for the separation of church and state. Or does it? And if it does, what does that separation mean?

Growing up in Massachusetts, I never thought to ask such questions. After all, we learned in school that thanks to its earliest settlers, our state was the very birthplace of religious liberty in America. And later, when I attended college, it was in Providence, Rhode Island, a city founded by separationist Roger Williams.

Later, though, I did wonder about church-state relations. Perhaps my interest was sparked when my daughter came home from her public school with a Bible presented to her there by a member of the Gideon Society. Or perhaps it began when I took her to a Christmas program at a public library and found myself listening to a passionately evangelical appeal aimed at six- and seven-year-olds.

Certainly, my interest was fully aroused by 1977, when I was elected to a term on the local school board. That interest grew as we debated how government funds might be apportioned between the public school and the town's parochial school. It grew as we discussed the use of public-school facilities by religious organizations. It became acute during the controversy raised when one group attempted to force the board to declare a Christian holiday an official public-school holiday.

By that time, of course, I knew that separation of church and state does not mean complete and absolute separation. The strands of politics and religion are wound together today, just as they have been throughout our history. I began to think about writing a book on the subject.

Then came Jim Jones and the tragedy of Guyana. The Christian-school movement. Public arguments over abortion, creationism, the Equal Rights Amendment, and other issues. The power of the so-called religious right. A book seemed more and more imperative.

Working on that book has been instructive. I learned that the early settlers of Massachusetts were not looking for religious liberty as we understand it and that the Constitution never mentions separation of church and state. I learned how complex church-state relations are, and how tempting it is to change position from issue to issue — to be a strict separationist in regard to government funding of religious institutions, for example, but to be less strict when it's a matter of regulating cults that appear to be dangerous or fraudulent. Most important, I became aware of the paradox in church-state relations. Government must be influenced by its citizens' moral and religious convictions. Yet it is, in the words of Thomas Paine, "of the utmost danger to society to make . . . [religion] a party in political disputes."

1. Church and State Today

Sundays in Ocean Grove, New Jersey, are pretty much like Sundays in any other American town or city.

Ocean Grove families can get into their cars on a Sunday morning and drive to church. In the afternoon, they can go to the movies or watch a ball game among neighborhood children. Youngsters may ride around on their bicycles. In summer, they can stroll the few blocks to the beach — the town is right on the Atlantic Ocean — to enjoy themselves. Citizens can even, if they wish, argue and quarrel with each other on Sunday.

It wasn't always like this in Ocean Grove. Until 1980, such Sunday activities were illegal for the people in the small community. Ball games and movies were not permitted. In fact, people were not allowed to assemble in public on Sunday for any nonreligious purpose. They could not ride bikes or drive cars — they could not even leave their cars parked in front of their own houses. Every auto had to be off the streets from 11:59 P.M. Saturday to 11:59 P.M. Sunday.

Ocean Grove's strict Sunday rules went back to

1869. That year, the New Jersey legislature gave the Ocean Grove Camp Meeting Association of the United Methodist Church the authority to make and enforce laws for the town. Camp Meeting leaders promptly passed a series of ordinances to ensure that Sunday would be a day of rest, one devoted entirely to religious activity. They appointed police officers to enforce their laws and set up a municipal court to deal with offenders. For over a century, that's the way things remained in Ocean Grove.

Then, in 1976, the Ocean Grove court found a man guilty of drunk driving. The man appealed his conviction on the grounds that a court established by a religious organization had no jurisdiction over his case. Three years later, the appeal came before the New Jersey Supreme Court, the state's highest court of law. That court ruled in the man's favor and overturned his conviction. By its ruling, the court took away much of the Camp Meeting Association's authority over nonreligious life in Ocean Grove.

The court held that the 1869 legislature had been wrong to give the Methodist group the power to make and enforce laws for the town. "The legislature . . . transformed this religious organization to Ocean Grove's civil government," the justices wrote. They criticized the nineteenth-century legislators for decreeing that "in Ocean Grove the church shall be the state and the state shall be the church," and pointed out that in Ocean Grove "government and religion are so inextricably intertwined as to be inseparable."

Church and state inseparable? Many Americans were surprised by the facts about Ocean Grove. Most of us assume that in the United States separation of church and state is the rule.

In many ways it is. In the United States breaking a religious law is not a criminal act. No public law forces anyone to donate to religious causes. People can worship as they want to — if they want to — but they do not have to. Decisions by the United States Supreme Court in the early 1960s put a legal end to Bible readings and the reciting of Christian prayers in the nation's public schools. In the court's opinion, institutions supported by federal, state, and local tax revenues cannot be used to promote a particular religion.

In some ways, the separation between church and state appears to be widening. At Christmastime, many cities display a Nativity scene in front of a public building. Recently, though, groups with names like Citizens Concerned for Separation of Church and State have gone to court to try to prevent municipalities from spending the thousands of dollars of public funds it costs to mount and maintain such crèches. Several suits have been handled by the American Civil Liberties Union (ACLU), an organization that has long supported the strict separation of church and state. The ACLU has also been involved in lawsuits aimed at banning the singing of Christmas carols in public schools. In some places, even without a court ruling, school boards have ordered an end to carol singing.

Occasionally, separation between church and state seems more like outright conflict. For example, the parents of a desperately ill child may refuse, for religious reasons, to allow the child to receive medical care. In such a case, attorneys for the state in which the child lives may step in and get a court to order treatment. Church-state conflicts can also come up when a religious group engages in what is considered to be illegal activity. On occasion, church members and leaders have been fined or imprisoned.

Yet how complete is separation of church and state in America, really? Belief in a supreme being is a cornerstone of American life and government, and most of us are so accustomed to that fact that we overlook it.

Every time we repeat the Pledge of Allegiance, we affirm that we are "one nation under God." We invoke God in our patriotic songs: "God Bless America," "America the Beautiful," "My Country 'Tis of Thee," "The Battle Hymn of the Republic." Whenever we use a piece of United States currency, either a coin or a bill, we proclaim that "In God We Trust." Meetings of Congress, state legislatures, and municipal bodies are opened by a chaplain's prayer. Chaplains paid out of public funds also serve in the armed forces and in prisons. Prayers are common at graduations and other school functions. In the nation's courts, witnesses usually take oaths on a Bible. Most businesses observe the Christian Sabbath.

Religion and civil life often mix. Public money frequently supports religious observances. If a pope visits the United States he may celebrate mass before huge crowds in a public park. Hundreds of policemen, paid out of the public purse, must be on hand to keep order. After the ceremony, park workers, also public employees, pick up after the throng. When Pope John Paul II was scheduled to stop in the heavily Catholic city of Boston in 1979, city officials first proposed paying for a $100,000 altar from which he would celebrate mass. Eventually, in the face of much protest, Boston authorities dropped their plan and the city's Catholic archdiocese paid for building the altar. The state of Massachusetts did, however, pass legislation giving all state employees a paid holiday on the day of the pope's visit.

Local, state, and federal governments offer financial aid, direct and indirect, to religion. Indirect support is available through tax laws. All buildings used for religious purposes — from temples and cathedrals to simple one-room meetinghouses — are exempt from property taxes. Direct financial aid comes in several forms. Taxpayers help pay the costs of the nation's many parochial, church-run, schools. Public monies, often in the form of social-service or medical-care payments, go to charities and hospitals operated by religious foundations.

Just as government is involved in religion, so organized religion is involved in government. Throughout our history, church groups have played a part in public affairs. In wartime, leaders of most faiths offer prayers for the success and safety of America's fighting men. During the Civil War, some clergymen prayed for the North, some for the South, and splits within religious denominations echoed the split within the country. Religious groups were also divided during the Vietnam War. Many priests, ministers, and rabbis supported the United States' military effort there, but others spoke out and demonstrated against the war.

Religious organizations have helped sway election results. In the presidential election of 1928, Republican Herbert Hoover faced Democrat Alfred E. Smith. Smith, a Roman Catholic, was the victim of an anti-Catholic campaign led by Protestants who claimed a Catholic president would run the country on orders from the pope. Smith lost the election. Thirty-two years later, John F. Kennedy, another Catholic candidate for president, was also the target of anti-Catholic propaganda. Kennedy, however, was narrowly elected.

State and local laws reflect religion's influence on government. Liquor laws are an example. In some communities, alcoholic beverages cannot be sold at all. In others, it is illegal to sell liquor within certain distances of a church. Some forbid the sale of beer and wine in grocery stores and supermarkets; others permit it. The hodgepodge of laws is a reminder of the long battle waged by numerous church groups against any sale or use of alcohol.

Although church groups have always been involved in our public life, the degree of their involvement has varied. Sometimes it has been greater, sometimes lesser.

Today is a time of increasing involvement. Religious groups seek to affect lawmaking in many areas. When, in 1973, the Supreme Court ruled it legal for pregnant women to obtain abortions, Americans opposed to abortion began trying to get new laws to limit, or end, the practice. Many antiabortionists carry on their work through religious organizations. Religious groups have come out in favor of other proposed laws — laws aimed at discouraging divorce, for instance, or forbidding the teaching of sex-education courses in public schools. Some groups want to censor school textbooks and library materials, or to force public-school teachers to instruct students in "creationism," the story of the beginning of life as it is told in the Bible.

Religious leaders continue to involve themselves in election politics as well. Churchmen do not hesitate to endorse — or oppose — candidates for office on the grounds of the candidates' attitudes toward abortion, homosexuality, and other matters. A growing number of clergymen are urging their parishioners and followers to vote as a group in order to elect politicians who promise to turn their particular religious beliefs into law for the entire country.

A great many Americans are dismayed by the kind of religious involvement in politics that we are seeing today. They believe the nation must maintain a solid wall between church and state. Anything less than complete separation, they say, violates one of our most cherished national principles.

2. Intolerance to Tolerance

The story of the English separatists — America's Pilgrims — is a familiar one. The separatists held religious views that differed from the official views of the Church of England, the Anglican church. In the England of the early 1600s, Anglicanism was the established religion. It was the state church; the monarch was its head, and anyone who disputed its doctrines, or who persisted in worshiping in non-Anglican churches, could be fined or imprisoned by the king's officers.

The separatists, however, knew of one European nation, Holland, that did allow freedom of religion. In 1608, a small band of separatists from the town of Nottingham sailed across the English Channel to Amsterdam. Later they moved to Leiden.

The separatists found both religious liberty and material prosperity in Leiden. But as time passed, they also saw their children taking on Dutch ways, and they did not like that. Determined to remain English, the separatists returned home in the summer of 1620.

Early in September, they began the long voyage to the New World to establish an English colony.

Everyone knows of the hardships of that voyage. Storms and fierce gales blew the *Mayflower* far north of its planned route and the bitter cold of the North Atlantic caused much suffering among the ship's 102 passengers. Several died. Finally, sixty-six days after leaving England, the *Mayflower* came within sight of land. A month later, on a bleak December day, the Pilgrims stepped ashore at what was to become Plymouth, Massachusetts. They were weak and hungry, exhausted and ill, but heartily thankful. At last they had what they had sought so long: religious freedom.

The story is familiar — but not entirely accurate. The Pilgrims did not find religious freedom in America. They weren't even looking for it. What they were looking for — and what they got — was the chance to establish their own official church, their own state religion. The Pilgrims lived in the New World much as they had in the Old, in a community where church law was enforced by the state. The difference was that this time it was *their* church and *their* state.

The Plymouth settlers drew up town laws aimed at producing religious conformity. For example, they thought celebrating Christmas was a sinful custom — they labeled Christmas festivities "popish" or "pagan" — and their laws reflected that belief. Christmas was just another working day in Plymouth and no one, no matter what his or her private feelings might be, was permitted to observe the holiday.

Strict as Plymouth's laws were, they were mild compared to those of nearby Boston, which was settled by the Puritans in 1630. The Puritans' religious beliefs were similar to the Pilgrims', but their way of life was far more rigid. Unlike the Pilgrims, the Puritans granted civil rights only to church members. People who did not belong to to the church could neither vote nor hold public office in the town.

In Boston, anyone who preached outside the church could be fined and banished from the colony. Banishment was a severe punishment. There were few towns in New England in the 1630s, and banishment meant going into the wilderness and trying to survive its harsh conditions. A few years after the religious dissenter Anne Hutchinson was forced to leave Massachusetts, she and most of her children were massacred by Indians. Their deaths were the work of "God's hand," according to one leading Puritan. In other cases, the Puritans carried out the work with their own hands. Boston Quakers were executed for their beliefs as late as 1661.

Religious intolerance was a hallmark of nearly all the early American colonies. Throughout the South, in Georgia, North and South Carolina, and Virginia, Anglicanism was the established religion. Virginia's "Lawes Divine, Moral and Martial," proclaimed in

1612, made death the penalty for speaking "impiously" of the Christian faith or for "blaspheming [cursing] God's holy Name." A person who would not, or could not, abandon the habit of swearing also could be put to death. So could anyone who broke the Sabbath. Whippings were due those who showed disrespect to a minister, failed to attend church, or refused to submit to an "examination in the faith."

In New York, which was the Dutch colony of New Netherland until 1664, Governor Peter Stuyvesant established the Dutch Reformed church as the state religion. Under Stuyvesant, Lutherans, Baptists, Quakers, Catholics, and Jews were actively persecuted.

The intolerance of the early colonists stemmed from intolerance in Europe and had roots that went back hundreds of years in European history. During the first years of the Christian era, paganism was the religion of the Roman Empire, which stretched from England in the west to the Persian Gulf in the east. For three centuries, Christians were persecuted wherever they appeared in the empire.

Then, in the year 311, the Roman emperor Constantine announced that henceforth Christians would be allowed to practice their religion in peace. Christianity flourished and began replacing paganism as Rome's official religion. Emperors ordered and paid for the construction of fine large church buildings, and worshiped in them publicly. Christian festivals became legal holidays.

For a time, Christians and pagans lived peacefully together under Roman rule, each group worshiping according to its beliefs. Early Christian leaders encouraged this spirit of tolerance. Freedom of conscience is a basic human right, they said.

But Christian ideas changed as Christianity spread and grew stronger. By the end of the fourth century, churchmen were arguing that Christians could not tolerate the existence of any other religious creed. Their reasoning was simple. Not to follow the teachings of Christ was a sin. Non-Christians would inevitably suffer the eternal torments of hell. Therefore, the church had a moral duty to convert nonbelievers, by force if necessary.

So religious intolerance took hold once more, and this time it was the Christian church that was doing the persecuting. What began as genuine concern for the welfare of people's immortal souls quickly turned into harsh religious repression. Nor did church leaders persecute only pagans. Anyone, even a Christian, whose opinions did not agree exactly with official church doctrines faced discipline. Men and women learned that they must abide by church teachings and church laws or take the consequences: financial ruin, imprisonment, torture, death.

The consequences might be meted out by religious leaders, but they were equally likely to come from the authorities of the state. Europe's secular rulers — its kings, princes, and dukes — showed themselves willing to back up church authority with all the power at their command. Again, their reasoning was simple. The state was charged with punishing those who committed crimes like theft and murder, crimes that affect the earthly body. But religious crimes like blasphemy and heresy (denying the truth of church teachings) can destroy the very soul itself, they believed, and are therefore worse even than murder. No wonder governments were eager to help stamp them out.

At the same time that secular governments were enforcing church laws, the church was lending its moral authority to the kings and queens of Europe. Coronations were religious ceremonies, and rulers made it clear that they governed by divine right. Churchmen, from mighty popes and cardinals to humble village priests, supported the rulers' claims and involved themselves deeply in national and international politics.

The union between church and state strengthened both. Obedience to God was obedience to the king and vice versa. Disobedience to either meant punishment on earth and throughout all eternity. Religious dissent was also treason. Taxes collected by the king paid for church, as well as court, expenses. Kings grew rich and so did members of the clergy. For centuries, the Church of Rome, the Catholic church, dominated European life and European politics.

Yet changes were on the way. In about 1380, an English priest named John Wyclif translated the Bible into English, making it directly available to people who could not read or understand Latin. Shortly afterward, the Czech priest John Huss translated some of Wyclif's own writings into his native tongue. The idea that ordinary men and women should be able to read Christ's teachings and apply them to their own lives was growing. Then, in 1517, Martin Luther publicly attacked the Catholic church by nailing a list of grievances to the door of a church in Wittenberg, Germany. The Protestant Reformation had begun.

The Reformation was not one movement, but several. In Germany, Luther's ideas led to the formation of a Lutheran church. In Geneva, Switzerland, John Calvin founded Calvinism, a sect that deeply influenced the English and American Puritans. Scottish John Knox was responsible for the beginnings of Presbyterianism. In England, King Henry VIII broke with the Church of Rome and established the Church of England in its place.

Although the leaders of the various Protestant sects rejected many of Catholicism's teachings and practices, few questioned one basic assumption of the Catholic church. That was the idea that church and state must work hand in hand to enforce both religious and civil law.

Some Protestants took this idea even further. In Geneva, Calvin set up a strict church-state, or theocracy. (*Theocracy* comes from the Greek words for "God" and "rule.") Calvin believed that if a community fails to obey God's laws it brings the wrath of the Almighty down upon itself. A community that lives in harmony with God's will, on the other hand, can expect the blessings of peace and prosperity. Therefore, Calvin concluded, *for its own good* the state must never tolerate the slightest religious dissent. Only if secular authorities, as well as religious ones, persecute dissenters, can they ensure a good and prosperous life for all. Or, as Calvin put it, "The punishments executed upon false prophets, and seducing teachers, do bring down the showers of God's blessings upon the civil state."

This notion — that civil government thrives with religious intolerance — came to America with many of its early settlers, and helps explain why there was so little tolerance in the colonies. Still, not all who came to the New World shared Calvin's point of view about church-state relations. One person who did not was a young separatist minister named Roger Williams.

Williams arrived in Plymouth in the year 1631, and promptly began quarreling with the authorities in Boston. Williams criticized the Puritans on two counts: for failing to break utterly with the Church of England as the separatists had, and for treating the Massachusetts Indians unfairly. But what really enraged the Puritans was Williams's contention that church and state should operate quite apart from one another.

In Williams's view, God created two separate and distinct spheres of life. The world of Nature is the political, civil sphere. The world of the Spirit is the religious one. The two can never mix.

This belief led Williams to a further conclusion. Men and women must be free to worship as they please. If Nature and Spirit are separate, religious matters lie strictly between individuals and their God. No outsider, neither king nor governor nor minister, can interfere.

To the Puritans, who had deliberately patterned Boston after John Calvin's theocratic Geneva, Williams's views were sinful and dangerous. They ordered him to back down, but Williams would not. The quarrel grew.

It came to a head in 1634. By then, New England's Indians were beginning to ally themselves with the French in Canada and to threaten English settlements. Fearful that some of their people might side with the French and Indians, Boston authorities ordered everyone in Massachusetts to take an oath of loyalty.

Williams refused. For the civil government to require the swearing of an oath in the name of God was to mix the natural world with the world of the spirit. Williams maintained that no government had the right to force such a religious action upon anyone.

The Puritans' response was to put Williams on trial before the General Court of Massachusetts. The court pronounced sentence of banishment in the fall of 1635, and in January Williams fled south to the shores of Narragansett Bay. There he established what is now Providence, Rhode Island.

Williams called Providence his "lively experiment." He wanted to demonstrate that men and women of different religions could live and work together in harmony. Even "popish and Jewish consciences" were welcome in Providence, and it was just a few miles away, in Newport, that the country's first synagogue was built.

In his determination to separate church from state, Roger Williams was ahead of his time. It would be decades before most other Americans adopted his ideas about religious freedom and began loosening the ties between religion and government.

Massachusetts did not get around to granting religious freedom to "all Christians (except Papists)" until 1691. What that boiled down to was religious freedom for Protestants only. Religious laws in Connecticut and New Hampshire echoed those of Massachusetts.

Tolerance was greater in New York. When the English Duke of York took over the colony from the Dutch, he gave each town the power to choose its own — Protestant — minister. The ministers were paid, and church buildings erected, from funds collected by secular authorities. Catholics and Jews were permitted to live and worship in New York, but unlike Protestants, they had to bear their own religious expenses. Catholics could not become citizens unless they renounced their allegiance to the pope in Rome.

Pennsylvania, founded by the Quaker William Penn, was likewise more tolerant than most of New England. Under the constitution Penn wrote in 1676, Jews and other non-Christians could live within the colony but could not vote or hold office. Those rights were reserved for "persons who profess to believe in Jesus Christ."

Maryland, often cited for its tolerance, was not actually as liberal as many suppose. The colony's original charter demanded that residents believe in the Trinity of God the Father, Jesus the Son, and the Holy Ghost. Maryland was founded by a Catholic, George Calvert, Lord Baltimore, and this Trinitarian formula opened the door to both Catholics and Protestants. However, it excluded Jews, atheists, and unitarian Christians (who believe that God exists as a single being). Within a few years, Catholics, too, were excluded from Maryland. In 1688, Anglicanism became the colony's official religion and Catholic settlers were no longer permitted to enter Maryland. Catholics already living in the colony were not allowed to worship there in public.

Anglicanism was the established religion throughout the Southern colonies. Its ministers were government employees. Their salaries were paid out of tax revenues, and many received valuable land grants from the king's officers. Dissenters were treated harshly. In Virginia, up until the 1770s, Baptist preachers could be arrested, whipped, and fined. Some were imprisoned and kept on a diet of bread and water. Virginians who denied the Trinity could be thrown into jail and their children taken from them. In North Carolina and South Carolina, people were required to agree that the Bible is divinely inspired, and South Carolina also enforced a belief in heaven and hell.

That was the picture in the colonies on the eve of the American Revolution. Tolerance was widespread, although some places were more tolerant than others. But nowhere, except in Rhode Island, was there true religious liberty or real separation of church and state.

3. Tolerance to Freedom

The American Revolution began in 1775 with the battle of Lexington and Concord and ended six and a half years later with the surrender of General Charles Cornwallis at Yorktown. The formal peace treaty between England and the new United States was signed on February 3, 1783. The thirteen colonies had become the thirteen states.

Thirteen not-very-united states. While they were fighting the English, the states shared a vital common goal. Cooperation was absolutely necessary. But with the war over, the states began going their separate ways, each one acting in its own selfish interests.

New York placed heavy taxes on ships from Connecticut and New Jersey. New Jersey struck back by taxing a New York lighthouse. Virginia and Maryland bickered about oyster fishing in Chesapeake Bay. Virginia also carried on a running argument with Pennsylvania and Delaware over their use of Virginia waters. By 1786, it seemed possible that the United States might collapse into complete disunity. It was obvious that the nation needed a central government strong enough to bind the states together and make them work as one country.

So, in May 1787, representatives from the states gathered in Philadelphia to begin writing a federal constitution. For four months, the delegates to the Constitutional Convention discussed how Americans would choose their leaders, who would be permitted to serve in Congress, what powers the president should have, how the courts would work — and what place religion would take in the new government.

From the start, it was clear that the day of official religions and government intolerance was just about over in America. Of the fifty-five convention delegates, an overwhelming majority opposed the setting up of an official national church.

There was a sound practical reason for this. By 1787 America was already a land of many faiths. True, most people were Protestants (of a population of approximately four million, about twenty-five thousand were Catholic and fewer than ten thousand Jewish), but America's Protestant sects covered a wide range, from high-church Anglicanism to the simplicity of the Mennonites and Quakers. Any attempt to turn a single sect into the official church would surely have led to bloodshed and civil war.

But the delegates favored religious liberty and separation of church and state for more than practical reasons. Many deeply believed that all men (though not women and not Indians or black slaves) are born with a natural right to freedom of conscience. Freedom of conscience is a God-given right and cannot be taken away by any law of man. This belief led the delegates to reject religious intolerance — and religious tolerance as well.

That sounds like a contradiction, but it is not. The word *tolerance* comes from a Latin word that suggests something that must be borne or endured. The delegates knew that when a government *endures* religious dissent, or *bears up under* the presence of Quakers, Catholics, Jews, Mohammedans, or atheists, its people are not truly enjoying freedom of religion. After all, what seems tolerable at one time may not at another, and a state that permits dissent one year may not allow it the next. Tolerance offered by a government can be taken away by that government. As one delegate, James Madison of Virginia, noted, "The right of every man is to liberty — not toleration." It was liberty — religious and political — that the men in Philadelphia were determined to preserve.

One question concerning religion came up early in the convention proceedings, when Benjamin Franklin of Pennsylvania suggested that "henceforth prayers imploring the assistance of Heaven, and its blessing on our deliberations, be held in this Assembly every morning before we proceed to business." Franklin's words were received in silence. No one wanted to embarrass the eighty-one-year-old statesman, or to hurt his feelings, but few of the delegates wanted daily prayers, either. They adjourned without acting on the motion.

The delegates' desire to keep formal religion apart from government was apparent throughout the convention. Whereas the Declaration of Independence refers to "Nature's God," the "Creator," the "Supreme Judge of the World," and "divine Providence," the Constitution makes no mention of God whatsoever (unless you count the phrase "In the year of our Lord one thousand seven hundred and eighty-seven"). The omission was not accidental but deliberate.

The delegates also took care to see that no one would be barred from holding federal office because of religious convictions. According to the third paragraph of Article VI, "No religious test shall ever be required as a qualification to any office or public trust under the United States."

This clause was the work of Charles Pinckney of South Carolina. Pinckney feared that without it, people of certain faiths might be kept from participating in the federal government as they were in the governments of several states. His proposal got the support of James Madison, who argued that if the clause were adopted, no one could ever claim that religious tests were acceptable because they were not specifically forbidden.

The clause went into the Constitution with little debate.

Another of Pinckney's motions fared less well. His proposal for a clause to forbid congressional interference in religious matters won almost no backers.

Few delegates thought such a clause was needed. James Madison believed it was so obvious government should stay out of religious affairs that it did not need saying. A New York delegate, Alexander Hamilton, went further, suggesting it might be dangerous to include Pinckney's proposed clause. Forbidding the government to act in one way might create the impression that it was permitted to act in another, slightly different way, Hamilton warned. Congress, for instance, might assume that although it could not get involved in religious disputes, it could legislate certain religious observances. This argument carried the day.

Some, however, continued to doubt the wisdom of leaving a freedom-of-religion clause out of the Constitution. When the convention finished its work and the Constitution was ready for signing, Virginian George Mason balked. He would not put his name to a document that did not guarantee religious liberty and the separation of church and state. These principles needed to be spelled out in the Constitution, Mason believed, not just implied in it.

As it turned out, the American people agreed with

Mason. When the Constitution went to the states to be ratified — formally agreed to — several states hesitated. They were reluctant to adopt a constitution that made no provision for freedom of religion and other fundamental freedoms. Two states, Rhode Island and North Carolina, refused outright to ratify. Six others ratified but simultaneously submitted proposals for a bill of rights to guarantee religious liberty, freedom of speech, the right to a fair trial, and so on. Thomas Jefferson, who was out of the country and did not take part in the Constitutional Convention, sent his friend Madison a letter about his reaction to the Constitution. After praising much of it, Jefferson went on, "I will now add what I do not like. First, the omission of a bill of rights providing clearly . . . for freedom of religion . . ."

Despite the doubts, nine states did ratify and the Constitution went into effect on March 4, 1789. George Washington was sworn in as president and the members of the first Congress took their seats. Right away they began working on amending the Constitution by adding a bill of rights.

It was Congressman James Madison, convinced by now that a bill of rights really was needed, who wrote its first draft. He wasted no time in addressing the question of religious rights. The opening words of the First Amendment, "Congress shall make no law respecting an establishment of religion," were intended to guarantee the separation of church and state. The next words, "or prohibiting the free exercise thereof," aim to ensure the right of all Americans to worship according to their individual beliefs. The amendment goes on to guarantee freedom of speech and of the press; freedom to assemble peacefully; and freedom to take action against government injustice, to sue for "redress of grievances." By linking these various freedoms in a single amendment, the nation's leaders demonstrated their conviction that political and religious liberty are two sides of the same coin and that neither one can exist without the other.

Congress passed the Bill of Rights on September 25, 1789, and immediately sent it to the states. Ratification was quick, and the bill became part of the Constitution in December.

But ratification did not end the debate over the First Amendment. For nearly two centuries, Americans have disagreed about what the amendment actually says about religious freedom and the separation of church and government. They have argued — are still arguing — about what the men who framed the amendment intended it to accomplish.

One argument centers on the phrase, or rather the missing phrase, *separation of church and state.* Nowhere in the amendment, or in the Constitution as a whole, do these words appear.

Some argue that their absence shows the men who

wrote the Constitution and the Bill of Rights didn't really want separation at all. One twentieth-century writer, James M. O'Neill of Brooklyn College, author of books on religion and the Constitution, has called the separation principle "spurious." "There is no such great American principle and there never has been," O'Neill wrote. J. Howard McGrath, United States attorney general under President Harry S Truman, declared that when the Supreme Court made legal decisions in favor of separation, it "distorted" the First Amendment. Supreme Court Justice William O. Douglas felt that "the First Amendment . . . does not say that in every and all respects there shall be a separation of Church and State." More recently, another member of the Court, Justice William H. Rehnquist, wrote that the First Amendment does not require the "insulation" of government institutions, such as schools, from church influences.

Does the omission of the words *separation of church and state* actually mean that separation was not what the Founding Fathers had in mind? Of course not, answer most American historians, lawyers, religious leaders, and political scientists. They point to other "missing phrases" in the constitution. There's no reference to a bill of rights, for instance, and the words *fair trial* do not appear. Yet we have a bill of rights, and people accused of crimes have a constitutional right to a fair trial.

It was Thomas Jefferson who first used the term *separation of church and state*. Writing to a group of Connecticut Baptists in 1801, Jefferson referred to his "sovereign reverence" for the Americans who adopted the First Amendment, "thus building a wall of separation between church and state." Although Jefferson did not take part in writing the Constitution and the Bill of Rights, he was in close touch with the men who did, and he knew what was in their minds. The First Amendment calls for separation, even though it does not use the word.

Other arguments about the First Amendment concern a word that *is* in the amendment. That word is *Congress*. The First Amendment is the only one in the Bill of Rights that mentions Congress. The other nine amendments simply state that certain actions may or may not be taken or that Americans are to enjoy this or that freedom. The Second Amendment, for example, says that "the right of the people to keep and bear arms shall not be infringed." That means, many people believe, that neither Congress nor the president nor the courts can keep Americans from owning guns.

As a matter of fact, Madison originally wrote the First Amendment in the style of the other nine. His first draft read, "The civil rights of none shall be abridged on account of religious belief, nor shall any national religion be established, nor shall the full and equal rights of conscience in any manner or on any pretext be infringed." But Congress debated the bill before passing it, and during that debate Madison's words were altered. By the time a vote was taken, the word *Congress* had slipped into the First Amendment.

Remember how Alexander Hamilton argued at the Constitutional Convention against Charles Pinckney's proposed clause on religious laws? Now we can see why. The First Amendment says what Congress cannot do. What about presidents and the courts, though? The amendment does not forbid either to act in religious affairs. By specifying something Congress *cannot* do, it implies what others *may*.

Our presidents call upon Americans to perform certain religious acts, such as observing days of prayer and thanksgiving. President Ronald Reagan had been in office just a few hours when he asked Americans to go to church to offer thanks for the release of fifty-two Americans who had been held hostage in Iran for 444 days. Only two presidents, Thomas Jefferson and James Madison, believed that the First Amendment made it impossible for them to proclaim religious holidays.

What's more, although the First Amendment says Congress cannot establish one religion or prohibit the practice of another, it does not prevent Congress from passing *any* kind of law that can affect religion. That has left Congress free to provide tax exemptions for religious groups, to give federal money to help support parochial schools, to permit the mailing of religious materials at special low postage rates, and so on.

A third ambiguous feature of the First Amendment is that, as written, it applies only to the federal government. It makes no mention of state and local governments and their relationship to religion. Even after the Bill of Rights became part of the Constitution, states were free to establish official religions, demand religious tests for office, and limit the civil rights of dissenters.

When the Constitution went into effect, four states, Massachusetts, Connecticut, New Hampshire, and Maryland, still maintained religious establishments. In those states, every taxpayer was required to contribute to religious organizations, although individuals could choose which church or group they wanted their money to go to.

Other vestiges of colonial attitudes toward religion remained in the United States. New Hampshire Catholics were not allowed to vote until 1851. Seventeen years later, the New Hampshire constitution still barred non-Protestants from state office, as North Carolina's did non-Christians. (The North Carolina provision was largely ignored, however, and a Jew was elected to the state legislature as early as 1808.) New Jersey did not officially extend full civil rights to non-Protestants until 1844. Only after 1868, when the nation adopted the Fourteenth Amendment to the federal

Constitution, did the First Amendment become legally binding upon the states.

The Fourteenth Amendment is one of three ratified just after the Civil War and intended to protect the civil rights of America's former slaves. It provides that no state shall "deprive any person of life, liberty, or property." Over the years, the Supreme Court has ruled that the "liberty" of the Fourteenth Amendment includes the religious liberty of the First. In effect, the Court says that the First Amendment should be regarded as saying: "Congress *and the state legislatures* shall make no law respecting an establishment of religion, or prohibiting the free exercise thereof."

One final point about the First Amendment. Although its aim may seem to be to limit religion's role in American life, its framers had no such intention in mind. Nowhere does the amendment say that government cannot show friendship and support for religion. In fact, the idea that religious feeling is necessary in a healthy society underlies the entire Constitution.

The Founding Fathers wanted to establish a system of fair and just laws. To do that, they believed they must model their civil law on the "natural law" of a supreme being, or a universal creator. Most of them believed in such a creator, although not all thought of God as specifically Christian. When the Founding Fathers banned religious tests for office and carefully separated church and state, they were trying not to exclude religion but to protect it. "Religion," said James Madison, "flourishes in greater purity, without than with the aid of government."

Madison was correct. Separating religion from government did allow it to flourish, and America has always been a deeply religious nation. As the pioneers pushed westward, churches were among the first buildings they erected in each new town. Missionaries braved the wilderness to bring the word of God to settlers and Indians alike. In the cities of the East, clergymen welcomed thousands of immigrants, helped them find homes and jobs, provided schools for their children, hospitals for their sick, and charity for their needy.

Visitors to the United States have been struck by this nation's great interest in religion. According to a Frenchman, Alexis de Tocqueville, who toured America in 1830, "There is no country in the world in which the Christian religion retains a greater influence over the souls of men than in America." Sixty years later, the English diplomat James Bryce noted, "The influence of Christianity seems to be . . . greater and more widespread in the United States than in any part of western Continental Europe, and I think greater than in England."

Today, that religious feeling is still strong — and apparently growing stronger — in America.

4. Church, State, and School

Molly is a tenth grader at St. Mary's High School. St. Mary's is a private, parochial school, owned and run by Molly's church. It offers students a wide variety of courses in English, social studies, science, math, foreign languages — and church doctrine. Yet St. Mary's is supported in part by public money from local, state, and federal governments.

Town money pays for Molly's bus rides to and from St. Mary's. In the school library are dozens of books purchased out of federal funds. Federal money also provides remedial teachers and materials for boys and girls who need the extra help. From the state comes money to pay for testing St. Mary's students in basic skills to see how they compare to high-schoolers in other systems. Molly's state gives $10 million a year to its private schools, most of which are church related.

In other words, government at all levels is subsidizing Molly's parochial-school education. Her religious training — and the religious training of millions of other American children in church-run elementary and secondary schools — is partially paid for through taxes collected from Americans of all faiths and creeds.

Is that constitutional? Does it violate the First Amendment prohibition against the establishment of a religion supported out of the public treasury?

Many Americans say it does. In 1961, shortly after he became president, John F. Kennedy asked Congress to pass a bill to provide more than $2 billion to the nation's schools over a three-year period. Kennedy emphasized that the money would go only to public elementary and high schools. He went on record as believing it is unconstitutional to spend government money on religious schools.

The president's plan quickly ran into trouble in Congress and within a year it was defeated. Much of the opposition came from church leaders who demanded that parochial-school children get their "fair share" of any federal funds for education.

Four years later, a new president, Lyndon B. Johnson, submitted another federal-aid-to-education bill. Unlike the Kennedy proposal, the bill Johnson sent to Congress provided for funds for private and parochial schools as well as for public ones. That set off new arguments in the Capitol and around the country. On one side were "separationists," who think church and state ought to operate completely apart from each other. On the other were "accommodationists," who believe it is the duty of government to accommodate —

cooperate with or oblige — the nation's religious institutions.

Separationists and accommodationists in Congress debated for two months before reaching a compromise and passing the first federal-aid-to-education law. Formally entitled the Elementary and Secondary Education Act, the law gives aid to public schools and offers private and parochial schools federal money to help them provide certain services to their students. Under the compromise, local school officials have some of the responsibility for deciding how public and private schools will share federal-aid-to-education money. Local officials also have to help determine how state and municipal education funds will be used in their communities. Therefore, the debate between separationists and accommodationists continues locally as well as on the state and federal levels.

Separationists see any government aid to parochial schools as a violation of the First Amendment. What is the difference between such aid, they ask, and the tax the Southern colonists of the seventeenth and eighteenth centuries had to pay to maintain the Anglican church? Or the money New Englanders were forced to contribute to the support of their Puritan (later Congregational) churches? Or the funds collected in New York to support a variety of Protestant establishments? No difference at all, is the separationists' answer.

Nonsense — there's a vast difference, the accommodationists reply. The aid that church-run schools get today is aid that benefits students, not the schools themselves, and certainly not a church. Students are getting the subsidized bus rides and are learning through the remedial programs. Students are reading the library books bought with taxpayer money. Students take the tests that aim to make their education comparable to that offered in public schools.

The separationists reject this argument. Students may be the ones reading the books, they point out, but it certainly benefits a school to have a large library, especially one that comes free. A school also saves by not having to provide its own bus service or testing programs.

Accommodationists have an answer for that, too. Even if getting public money does help a parochial school, they say, that help has nothing to do with religion. Remedial programs teach math and reading, not theology. Library books bought with government money must be about nonreligious subjects; the government has made that plain to parochial-school administrators. Government funds are used by parochial schools to help cover the costs of secular programs, not religious ones.

Separationists don't accept that argument because it is clear to them that any money a parochial school does not have to spend on secular teaching is freed for its religious program. Suppose a parochial school has

$500 of church money available for new library books. School officials plan to spend half the sum on nonreligious fiction and nonfiction and half on theological works. If the federal government comes along and offers the school an additional $250, the school can buy secular materials with that and double its expenditure on religious publications. The government is helping the school in its religious function, even if that help is indirect.

What's more, separationists say, government aid to religious schools tends to help some religions more than others. One that benefits especially is the Roman Catholic church. About two thirds of all American religious elementary and secondary schools belong to the Catholic church. Of the slightly over four million American children in church-run schools, more than three million attend Catholic schools. (That explains why the word *parochial* seems to be a synonym for *Catholic*. Actually the word means "parish," and a parochial school is any school owned by a religious group and intended to give students a religious, as well as a secular, education.)

Another reason the Catholic church benefits so much from parochial-school aid is that Catholic-school administrators have traditionally been more likely than Protestants or Jews to take advantage of whatever government money is available to them. In the past, few non-Catholic groups applied for government aid for their schools and colleges. These groups have held a separationist viewpoint, convinced that the First Amendment does prohibit such government aid. In return, they expect no government interference in the running of their institutions. During the 1961 debate over President Kennedy's aid-to-education bill, an official of the Lutheran church, which runs a parochial-school system of its own, came out flatly against any form of public support for church-run schools.

Today, that Protestant attitude seems to be changing. The past few years have seen a tremendous growth in the number of Protestant "Christian schools." These schools are owned and operated by Baptist churches, or by other conservative or "fundamentalist" religious groups, and their administrators are beginning to show an interest in some forms of government subsidy. Fundamentalist churches, therefore, must be counted along with the Catholic church as those that stand to benefit most from state aid to private schools.

And that, the separationists argue, amounts to a kind of establishment of religion. Using tax revenues to pay parochial-school costs is the same as levying a tax to help support Baptist and Catholic churches. It is unconstitutional under the antiestablishment clause of the First Amendment.

Not at all, accommodationists respond. On the contrary, it would be unconstitutional *not* to provide public support for parochial schools. They maintain that if government does not give parochial schools the funds they need to survive, it will jeopardize the religious freedom of millions of Americans.

Why? A church's parochial-school system is a vital part of that church's ministry. Take the Catholic school system. One writer on church-state relations, Richard E. Morgan, calls it "an important way in which the Church goes about its business of fishing for souls." Deprive the Catholic church of its schools and you deprive it of a major tool for carrying out its religious mission. Make it impossible for Catholic parents to obtain a Catholic-school education for their children — and this will happen if Catholic schools are forced to close for lack of money — and you are keeping those parents from observing their religion as they see fit. Fail to provide the government support Catholic schools need and you may be denying the free exercise of religion to forty-nine million American Catholics.

It's the same for Christian schools. Many Baptists, and members of other fundamentalist Protestant sects, send their children to Christian schools so they will get a good "moral" education. Boys and girls in Christian schools are taught in ways that reflect fundamentalist religious beliefs. In science class they learn about how God created the earth and the heavens in six days, not about Charles Darwin's theory of the evolution of plant and animal species. In English classes, they are more likely to read stories about religion and morality than contemporary literature. Bible lessons and instruction in creationism are what many fundamentalists want for their children, but such lessons are not available in public schools. If Christian schools cannot survive financially, fundamentalists will have lost the right to an education in keeping with their religious convictions.

Separationists reject this argument as well. Carried to its logical extreme, they say, it would oblige government to pay the entire cost of the secular and religious education of every fundamentalist in the country and of every Catholic, too. In fact, it would mean providing religious training for every child whose parents want it. That could include just about every child in the nation.

Separationists point to another possible consequence of continued public support for parochial schools —the effect that such support is likely to have on the nation's public schools.

Public support for private schools hurts public schools. Every dollar of local, state, or federal money that goes to a parochial school is a dollar that is not going to a public school. And public schools need every dollar they can get. They face rising costs: Teachers' salaries go up yearly, and so do the prices of heating oil, gasoline for school buses, electricity, books, paper, audio-visual equipment, telephone service, and so forth. Already, hundreds of public-school systems are in serious financial trouble.

That trouble will be worse in the future, if new

schemes for the public support of private schools go into effect. One plan calls for Congress to grant tax credits to parents of private-school children. This will permit people to deduct up to $500 per year from their income-tax payments if they have children in a private or parochial school. That's a big saving, and a real incentive for American parents to abandon public education.

Another idea for public financing of private schools is the voucher plan. Under it, parents would get a government voucher — a sort of blank check — to "spend" at the public or private school of their choice. Each school would send the vouchers received from parents to the state or federal government, which would then reimburse the school for each child's education. This plan, like tax credits, would surely be challenged in the Supreme Court. If the Court ruled it was constitutional, it would be bound to encourage parents to send their children to private and parochial schools. It would help those schools only at the expense of public ones.

Who would be most likely to suffer most from the weakening of America's public-school system? Most educators and social scientists agree it would be girls and boys from needy families or those who are black or belong to other minority groups. These children are most dependent upon the public schools for their education. Many Americans fear that government aid to parochial schools, especially to the fast-growing Christian-school system, will result in better education for white middle-class students and poorer education for minority students and for the urban poor of all races and nationalities. They predict it will produce private schools full of white faces and public schools full of darker ones.

Most civil rights leaders oppose the voucher plan and the tax credit plan. Dr. Eugene T. Reed of the National Association for the Advancement of Colored People stated that organization's position: "We are against aid [to private schools] in any way, shape, or form, because it only helps those who would skirt legislation on segregation."

Some church leaders agree. The Reverend Dean Kelley, of the National Council of Churches, which represents thirty-two Protestant and Eastern Orthodox denominations, is one of them. "Subsidizing private schools . . . [with] religious schools giving preference to their own members might succeed in carrying out . . . racial segregation with federal funds," he said.

Kelley and Reed are firm believers in freedom of religion. As far as they are concerned, Catholics, Baptists, Jews, and all others are free to give their children whatever kind of religious training they want. But they, like other separationists, do not accept the argument that eliminating public support for religious schools threatens anyone's liberties. Furthermore, they are unwilling to endanger America's public-school system by turning more and more public money over to private and parochial education.

Accommodationists believe in freedom of religion, too. But they believe freedom cannot be assured unless government does all it can to encourage and support religion.

Although accommodationists and separationists both believe in the First Amendment, the two groups see that amendment from different points of view. Separationists emphasize the amendment's opening words: "Congress shall make no law respecting an establishment of religion." Accommodationists stress the next clause: "or prohibiting the free exercise thereof."

The two clauses express a common goal — to protect Americans' religious liberties. At times, however, they come into conflict. The first part of the amendment prohibits any public support for religion. It says government must be absolutely neutral in church matters. The second part implies something other than strict neutrality. In forbidding the government to hinder the free exercise of religion, it hints that under some circumstances government may show positive support for religious institutions.

This conflict underlies arguments between separationists and accommodationists over state aid to parochial schools. It underlies other disagreements about church-state relations as well.

5. Taxes and Charities

"In this world nothing is certain but death and taxes," said Benjamin Franklin. But as far as America's religious institutions are concerned, Franklin was wrong. Taxes are not at all certain for them.

The nation's tax laws — local, state, and federal — are designed to favor institutions that serve the community. School buildings and college campuses, for example, are exempt from local property taxes. Donations to charitable organizations such as the Red Cross or the United Fund are not subject to income tax. Scientific and medical research foundations, nonprofit environmental groups, and consumer organizations also enjoy advantages under tax laws. But of all the institutions that profit from tax exemptions, religious groups benefit most.

Tax exemptions for churches fall into three categories. First are tax-free donations to religious organizations. Anyone who gives money to a church can subtract that sum from his or her total income before figuring out how much tax is owed. The larger the donation, the greater the tax saving, and that encourages people to give generously to the religion of their choice.

Another advantage for churches is that much of their real estate — land and buildings — is not taxed. According to one estimate, there is more than $80 billion worth of untaxed church property in the United States. New York City alone could raise an extra $35 million a year by taxing its church-owned real estate.

Religious institutions also benefit from laws that almost entirely exempt them from income taxes on the money they make in various business activities. This particular advantage is unique to religious groups. Unlike the law on donations or on property taxes, it does not apply to other nonprofit organizations, or to educational or research facilities.

How does the conflict between the antiestablishment clause and the free-exercise provision of the First Amendment apply to tax matters? Some people claim that the exemptions are unfair and unconstitutional because in granting them, government is making an establishment of religion. Saying that a church does not have to pay a property or income tax is the same as giving that church a gift of public money, they maintain. By permitting church property to go untaxed in New York City, officials there are giving city churches $35 million annually.

Of course the city can't afford to give up that $35 million altogether. The money has to come from somewhere, and "somewhere" turns out to be the pockets of New Yorkers. The taxpaying public makes up the $35 million by paying higher taxes than it would have to if the religious exemptions did not exist. New Yorkers, like everyone else in the country, are taxed extra to support religion. That does appear to be a direct violation of the first part of the First Amendment.

But the second part of the amendment makes it clear why Americans accept the "violation." To allow taxation of church income and real estate would be to place America's religions at the mercy of the state. Taxing religious organizations could make possible the very religious persecution the Founding Fathers tried to avoid.

Imagine that your neighborhood suddenly becomes the headquarters of a new church. Members of this church hold unconventional religious views. Perhaps they profess to believe in the occult, or in a mixture of Christianity and Eastern mysticism. They dress oddly, and roam the streets asking for handouts or selling novelty items. They hang around school yards and recreation centers seeking to convert the young people they meet.

It doesn't take long for townspeople to become upset. Parents don't want their children to join the new church and turn away from family and faith. Citizens are sick of being asked for money every time they appear downtown. Store owners don't like shoppers being bothered by church members. They fear customers will start taking their business where they can shop without being annoyed. Soon the whole town is demanding that the church be forced to close down.

How best to get it out of town? Tax it out. Slap higher and higher property taxes on any land or buildings the church owns. Deny church members tax-exempt status for their businesses. Tax their incomes to the hilt. Pretty soon the church will be gone.

The power to tax involves the power to destroy, Supreme Court Chief Justice John Marshall said a century and a half ago. He was right. If it had this taxing power, government could destroy our imaginary church and deprive its members of their freedom of religion. Unquestionably, tax exemptions for religious institutions must continue if we are to have freedom of religion.

Yet the exemptions raise problems. They are tantamount to outright gifts. And as with public aid to parochial schools, American tax laws benefit some churches more than others. Religious institutions that are rich and own lots of property — the Catholic, Episcopal, and Mormon churches, for example — can save millions of dollars a year. Other denominations, such as Jehovah's Witnesses and Pentecostal groups, which own little money or property, have less to gain from tax-exemption laws.

Another problem is that people may take unfair advantage of laws that protect church property and income from taxation. In some cases, people disgusted with high property taxes have sent away to "divinity schools" for quick, easy-to-pass correspondence courses. Hundreds of people from all walks of life now have diplomas showing they are "ministers" — and exempt from property taxes. In 1981, however, a New York court ruled mail-order religious exemptions illegal in that state.

Other people try to use religious exemptions to get around income-tax laws. In the mid-1970s, five Connecticut priests set up a tax-exempt mail-order business. In theory, income from the business went to charity, but in fact, the priests lived, overlooking scenic Long Island Sound, in a luxurious mansion complete with a private swimming pool and a garage full of expensive cars. Not surprisingly, the federal government questioned the business's tax-exempt status, and in 1980, the Postal Service took away its mailing permit, which had allowed the priests to ship their products at special low rates.

Federal authorities also questioned the tax exemptions of the Christian Brothers winery in California. The Christian Brothers are members of a monastery, but the wine and brandy they produce are on sale in supermarkets and liquor stores from coast to coast. For years, the brothers paid no income tax, and in the late 1950s, government tax collectors sued them in court for $3.5 million in back taxes. According to the government, the brothers were engaged in a profit-making business.

The brothers countered by asserting that their wine making was a sacerdotal activity (wine is used in the Catholic sacrament of communion) and hence protected under the First Amendment's free-exercise clause. The court, however, did not agree, and ordered the brothers to pay the taxes.

Even some religious leaders find fault with certain church tax exemptions. Eugene Carson Blake, past president of the National Council of Churches, deplores the fact that exemptions put so much of the tax burden on those who can least afford it, the poor. He fears that one day Americans may turn against their rich and powerful churches. "One hundred years from now," said Dr. Blake, "the present pattern of religious tax exemption . . . may present the state with problems of such magnitude that their only solution will be revolutionary expropriation of church property."

James A. Pike, the former Episcopal bishop of San Francisco, agreed. Pike believed that some churches have become too wealthy, too involved with money matters. "Worldly power has seduced the church from its spiritual concerns of the past," he contended. The American Jewish Congress (AJC), also concerned about religious exemptions that seem unfair, has begun making a yearly financial contribution to New York City in place of taxes on its Manhattan headquarters.

The AJC does not oppose all tax exemptions for religious institutions, any more than Dr. Blake or Bishop Pike. Certainly, all would favor exemptions on buildings actually used for worship, or on funds that go for religious work. But to them, exemptions on commercial real estate, or on a church's business income, are different. In their view, the free-exercise clause of the First Amendment does not require government to help religion out by exempting churches from almost all taxes.

Another church-state controversy that revolves around the conflicting themes of the First Amendment concerns social service programs. Traditionally, churches have run hospitals, orphanages, counseling centers, soup kitchens, and many other charities. The Catholic church has a particularly well organized and staffed welfare system.

But in the United States today, church welfare is not enough. Americans have become accustomed to a tremendous variety of social services, aid to dependent children, food stamps, free or relatively inexpensive medical care, foster care, social security for widows and orphans and the elderly, Head Start and day-care programs, subsidized school breakfasts and lunches — the list goes on and on. Only government, with its enormous taxing power, can afford it all. Yet few churches want to abandon their centuries-old charities.

The solution? Channel government social service

funds through church welfare facilities. Offer government funds for expansion programs at church hospitals. Pay church orphanages to care for parentless
children. Make it financially possible for religious institutions to continue their function of feeding the hungry, nursing the ill, and sheltering the homeless.

This solution has its advantages. It permits the government to help support religious institutions, and at
the same time, it lets churches help government and the
needy. Church welfare organizations are already in
place, so government does not have to waste time and
money constructing new public facilities. Often a
church can provide more care for less money, too. This
is especially true of Catholic institutions, which may be
staffed by members of religious orders rather than by
outside professionals who demand high salaries.

Yet there are drawbacks to this solution, drawbacks
like the First Amendment prohibition against establishment of a religion. What is giving state money to a
church-run orphanage or hospital but government support for the church? And again, although government
may not intend to favor one religion over another,
some churches do benefit more than others from government aid.

In 1946 a law called the Hill-Burton Act made $150
million in federal funds available for hospital construction. During the first four years the law was in effect,
the government made ninety-nine grants to hospitals

with religious affiliations. Of the ninety-nine hospitals, seventy-six were Catholic. In all, Catholic institutions received more than 80 percent of the funds given out to church-affiliated hospitals in those four years. The remaining 20 percent went largely to Episcopalian, Methodist, and Jewish hospitals.

But does it matter that Catholic hospitals benefited most under Hill-Burton? After all, Catholic hospitals were presumably giving the most service, too, since they so greatly outnumbered hospitals of other denominations. Unfortunately the kind of service they were giving did turn out to be a problem.

Soon after receiving one large Hill-Burton grant, St. Francis's Catholic hospital in Poughkeepsie, New York, ordered seven of its doctors to stop practicing there. The doctors were associated with Planned Parenthood, an organization that promotes family planning and birth control. The Catholic church regards birth control as morally unacceptable.

Suppose a non-Catholic woman were admitted to St. Francis. While in the hospital, in a wing built with federal money, the woman asks for information about methods of birth control.

St. Francis doctors refuse her request. They tell the woman that contraception is a sin and that it is up to God, not her, to decide how many children she will have.

Yet the woman's own religious convictions do allow

her to use birth control. In fact, she believes it would be wrong — morally wrong — for her to have more children than she and her husband want and can care for. Now she is being forced to accept religious dictates she does not believe in. And she is being forced to do so at government expense.

Could this really happen? In 1980, the Roman Catholic Archdiocese of New York, under a contract with New York City, took over responsibility for providing medical services at two city hospitals. As the contract took effect, church leaders announced that abortions — legal under law but condemned by the Catholic church — would no longer be performed at either hospital, nor would patients be given advice about contraception.

City officials reacted quickly. They reminded the archdiocese that it was receiving $2.25 million yearly in state welfare money. Under the state constitution, none of that money can go to a religious institution unless the institution acts in a purely nonreligious capacity. To force Catholic beliefs upon non-Catholics in a public hospital is not acting in a "nonreligious capacity." If New York permitted Catholic officials to follow their announced policy, they would be promoting the doctrine of one church and forcing the three-hundred-thousand-odd young women served by the two hospitals to adopt that doctrine as their own. That would violate the U.S. Constitution as well as the constitution of New York State.

Then should the city have ordered the archdiocese to compel its doctors to perform abortions? That would mean forcing Catholics to accept moral standards they do not believe in. It would mean forcing them to commit what they see as a mortal sin. That, too, would violate the First Amendment.

Eventually a compromise was reached. The archdiocese agreed to offer abortions and birth-control information at Lincoln and Metropolitan hospitals. But the services are available through independent staff members; no doctor or nurse connected with the archdiocese, or with its medical college, is involved.

Separationists seem satisfied with this compromise. But many would probably be happier if no compromise had been necessary, if government programs were not funded through religious institutions at all. That would not violate anyone's religious liberties, they believe, because people would still be free to appeal to charities run by their own churches. Keeping public money out of religious institutions, the strict separationists say, is the only way to be sure of avoiding an unconstitutional establishment of religion.

6. Rights in Conflict

Bang! Bang! Charles Williams was cleaning paint brushes in his uncle's Detroit neighborhood when he heard the shots. Perhaps Williams tried to take shelter; perhaps he did not have time. What is certain is that a bullet entered his shoulder and that he fell to the ground. He was rushed to a nearby hospital.

In the emergency room, the thirty-three-year-old Williams was met by a doctor who saw at once that although the wound was serious — a blood vessel near the heart had been cut as the bullet passed through — it would probably not be fatal. An operation would be necessary to repair the artery and Williams would need repeated transfusions to replace the blood he was losing. Even so, the doctor was "more than 90 percent certain" the patient would recover.

Six and a half hours later, Williams was dead — dead because he refused to permit doctors to give him the blood he needed. He belonged to a religious group, Jehovah's Witnesses, that prohibits transfusions. The Witnesses cite the Bible's book of Acts, chapter 15, verse 20 — ". . . abstain from pollutions of idols, and from fornication, and from things strangled, and from blood" — as the basis of their prohibition. Faithful to his convictions, the young man chose death. Making that choice, he created a tangle of legal and ethical problems.

A few days after the shooting, which took place in July 1980, two men were charged in the case. The two lived just down the street from the garage where Williams had been working. They had begun arguing, then quarreled fiercely. Each went into his house and returned armed with a gun. Blazing away at each other from opposite sides of the street, one fired wildly, hitting Williams. The two men were charged with murder.

Murder? A lawyer for one of the men argued that no murder had been committed. Instead, the Jehovah's Witness had chosen to die. "It's my position," the lawyer said, "that a person cannot arbitrarily refuse medical attention and die as a result and then have someone charged with his murder." In the view of many, Williams died because he refused medical care, not because he was shot. To convict those who fired the bullets would be to punish them for Williams's religious beliefs. And what if the shooting had taken place in a state with the death penalty for murder? If anyone were executed for a crime like this one, who would have caused whose death?

Of course, the accused men's rights could have been

protected by forcing the shooting victim to accept blood. The hospital might have requested an emergency court session and applied for permission to go ahead with transfusions. But if the court had granted permission, wouldn't it have been violating the patient's First Amendment right to practice his religion as he saw fit, without interference from the state? Surely, if separation of church and state means anything, it means government will not interfere in people's private religious beliefs.

Unfortunately it's not that simple. Many times one person's right to religious liberty comes into conflict with someone else's civil, religious, or moral rights. The Jehovah's Witness case is particularly dramatic, but the question it raises — to what extent may government curtail one liberty in order to preserve another? — is a question that comes up over and over in church-state relations. Often, as in this case, it arises over medical issues.

Jehovah's Witnesses are not alone in their attitude toward certain techniques of modern medicine. Other groups, notably members of the Church of Christ, Scientist, reject the concept of illness as something that requires medical treatment. Christian Scientists believe that what others call illness is nothing but an illusion that can be overcome through prayer and positive thinking. Healing comes from God, not man, and practicing Christian Scientists will have nothing to do with doctors, hospitals, or medicinal drugs. Members of some other religions, too, stay away from medicines and rely on faith to heal them when they are ill or injured.

For adults, such reliance can be defended. A mature man or woman who is sick by medical standards can claim the right to refuse treatment. If the patient is a child, though, it is a different matter.

Take the case of a three-year-old with cancer. Doctors say that without treatment the child will die. The parents are aware of the diagnosis, but their religious principles do not allow them to receive medical care and they deeply believe it would be wrong for their child to receive it either. Should the doctors take the parents to court, gain temporary custody of the child, and treat him? Should the parents be allowed to act on their convictions and condemn their child to death? Whose right is greater: a child's to life or an adult's to freedom of conscience?

Now suppose that a terminally ill cancer patient is severely mentally retarded, unable to walk or talk, doomed to live out his life in a vegetablelike state. Or suppose he is less retarded, but still unable to live a normal life. Should his parents be able to keep doctors from giving him life-saving medical care? In a recent Massachusetts case, the guardian of a retarded leukemia victim asked doctors to withhold treatment. But state authorities threatened a murder prosecution if the guardian stopped treatment and the patient died.

Another case involving death arose in New York State in 1979. In this instance the patient was a member of the Marianist Brotherhood, a Catholic religious order. Blind and comatose, eighty-three-year-old Brother Joseph Charles Fox lay in a Long Island hospital, kept alive by a mechanical respirator that did his breathing for him. Outside Brother Fox's hospital room, members of his religious community sought court permission to turn the respirator off so the old man could "die with dignity." Quoting Catholic church doctrine, the Marianists called the respirator "an extraordinary measure which need not be used to prolong life." Yet a New York district attorney made it clear that under the law he could ask for a murder indictment against anyone who did turn off the machine. The D.A. feared that if the law allowed a respirator to be turned off, it might one day allow "mercy killings" of patients with terminal illness or those who were in great pain. (Many doctors, of course, share this fear.) The district attorney acted on the assumption that Brother Fox's right to cling to life outweighed his right to death with dignity. Was he right?

Rights come into conflict over other life-or-death issues. Since 1973, when the Supreme Court overturned state antiabortion laws, abortion has been legal in this country. Not only that, but for a time, low-income women could receive abortions at public expense, through state and federal health-care programs. By the late 1970s, however, new state and federal laws limited the use of government money for abortion, and in 1980 the Supreme Court ruled in favor of these restrictive laws.

Should government condone — even pay for — abortions. The operation means taking the life of a fetus that would otherwise develop into a baby, a human being. Millions of Americans regard abortion as murder and believe it should be banned, by a constitutional amendment if necessary.

Other people see it differently. They think that only a woman herself has the right to decide whether to bear a child. This is particularly true when a pregnancy is the result of rape or incest, but in *any* case, they maintain, government should not tell a woman what to do about a matter as personal as her health.

Who is right: those who believe in a woman's "right to choose," or those who emphasize a fetus's "right to life"?

Closely related to the abortion issue is the matter of birth control. For many Americans, religious objections to abortion also apply to contraception. The Catholic church, for instance, links birth control, abortion, and the right to die. Birth and death are irreversible processes, the church says, and humans have no right to

interfere with either. Laws in several of the world's
Catholic nations limit people's right to obtain contra-
ceptives. Should similar laws be passed here?

Conflicts over people's religious rights is not limited
to life-or-death issues. They can crop up anywhere, in
schools, in industry — even in athletics.

One sports organization whose members helped stir
a conflict is the Oak Ridge, Tennessee, high-school
football team. Many Oak Ridge students and teachers,
including members of the team, are devout Christians.
Before every game, the team gathers on the field for a
prayer. Players pray during and after the game, too,
and before and after practice sessions.

Finally, an Oak Ridge lawyer, the father of a former
team member, objected. He alleged that it is against the
Constitution to require public-school students, some of
whom may not be devout Christians, or Christians at
all, to take part in prayer. The lawyer asked the school
board to order an end to religious observances on
school property or during school functions.

Should the board do as the lawyer asked? Or may
team members continue to pray together publicly?
Which right should government protect: one person's
right to worship or another's not to be forced to do
so?

Prayer is a volatile issue around the country. Until
the mid-1960s, students in public schools listened to a
Bible reading and repeated the Lord's Prayer every day.

Then the Supreme Court ruled it unconstitutional to force students in public, tax-supported schools to participate in the rituals of a particular faith. Bible reading and group praying are now illegal in public schools.

Many Americans deplore the court's decision and are mounting a strong movement to "get religion back into the schools." A 1980 Massachusetts law required public-school teachers to ask for student volunteers to lead each class in prayer. Anyone who did not care to take part could get up, leave the room, and stand outside in the corridor. A Kentucky law made it mandatory to post a copy of the Ten Commandments in every classroom in every public school in the state. And there have been several attempts to amend the Constitution to obligate schools to set aside time for "voluntary" prayer by teachers and students.

Should such an amendment be added to the federal Constitution? Should the Massachusetts and Kentucky laws be permitted to stand? Should government promote religious practices or try to keep them out of the nation's public institutions?

Rights come into conflict in other school-related matters. Not long ago, a New York dairy farmer named Thomas Hemple took his twelve-year-old daughter and eleven-year-old twin sons out of public school. Public schools "turn out mental and moral cripples," Hemple said, and he began teaching his children at home. School authorities, however, said the children were not learning well under their father's instruction, and ordered them back to class. A family court judge repeated the order, but Hemple would not promise to obey it. "I'm going to do what it tells me to do in the Bible," he told news reporters.

Should the court back up its order with a fine or a jail term for Hemple? Should it remove his children from his care, as courts have sometimes done in such cases? Whose right is greater: a child's to what the community considers a good education or a father's to exercise his religious beliefs?

Educational standards are at issue in other cases, especially since the sudden growth of the Christian-school system. Around the country, Christian-school officials are pressing for exemptions from state education standards. If exemptions are allowed, Christian schools (and other private and parochial schools) could hire teachers who do not meet any of the requirements for public-school teachers. School administrators could crowd as many pupils into each classroom as they wished and refuse to follow state curriculum guidelines for academic subjects. Schools might not even have to meet state health and safety standards.

Christian-school administrators argue that unless they win exemptions, their religious liberty is compromised. Staff members' religious beliefs are more important than their teaching credentials, the administrators say, because they are more like missionaries than teachers. They must continue to put missionary work first, the administrators say, if Christian schools are to teach fundamentalist religious beliefs to their students. Christian-school authorities also demand absolute freedom to decide what their student will read and study. If their boys and girls spend most of their time studying the Bible, and little or no time doing math or reading world history and literature, that is none of the state's business. For the state to set educational standards for Christian schools is to violate fundamentalists' religious rights.

Public-school officials, among others, dispute this. They believe government has an obligation to see that all the nation's children get a good, well-rounded education. The only way to make sure they do is to force parochial schools to conform to basic state education standards.

Which set of school officials is right? How much should the state interfere in Christian education?

How much should Christians interfere in state education? In many school districts, fundamentalists are demanding that students be taught creationism — the theory that God created the heavens and the earth in six days — along with Darwin's theory of evolution. Teaching evolution without creationism, they say, violates their children's religious rights.

Representatives of major faiths and most public-school officials object to including creationism in the science curriculum. Creationism is a religious belief, they maintain, and has nothing to do with science. Teaching it as part of a science course will confuse students about what science really is. In addition, public-school employees should not be required to teach the religious doctrines of any church.

Whose right should take precedence — a fundamentalist's to hear his point of view in class, or another's to study science unmixed with religious theory?

Another school issue is involved in the case of the Rebekah Home for Girls in Corpus Christi, Texas. The home was founded in 1957 by Lester Roloff, an evangelist minister with Old Testament ideas about sin and punishment. Roloff describes the girls in his home as "prostitutes, runaways, and dopers." Many were sent to him by their families, but their expenses were largely paid for through Roloff's "People's Church." Under Roloff's direction, the girls spent four hours a day studying religion and less time on academic subjects. They wore uniforms and gave up radio, television, rock music, coffee, soft drinks, and almost all make-up.

Roloff kept a close check on his girls. Their rooms were bugged and alarms were wired to each window. Mail was censored. Girls who broke the rules were "licked" with wooden paddles; those who tried to run away were put in solitary confinement for days at a time. People familiar with the home spoke of even worse physical and mental abuses.

Did social workers for the state of Texas have the right to go into the Rebekah Home and see what conditions were like? Roloff said no. The home was a branch of his church and churches are outside government control, he said.

State officials disagreed. They claimed that the girls at the Rebekah Home were treated more harshly than prisoners at most juvenile jails. Yet they were not convicted criminals, just teen-agers from troubled homes. "The state had a right to protect these kids," one former member of the state attorney general's staff said.

Another school issue involves segregation. During the 1960s and 1970s, the federal government made massive efforts to integrate America's public schools. Busing — transporting students from black neighborhoods to white schools and from white neighborhoods to largely black schools — is one of the most effective, and least popular, ways the government has found to integrate.

Resentment over "forced" busing is strong among many Americans. Both blacks and whites have worried about its inconvenience, about long pre-dawn and after-dark bus rides for children as young as five and six. Other people don't like the fact that children may be taken out of modern suburban schools and driven to dilapidated city schools. And some white parents plain don't like the idea of integration and think whites ought to stick with whites and blacks with blacks.

Whatever its cause, the resentment has led to the founding of thousands of so-called segregation academies — private schools with firm, but unwritten, "whites only" admission policies. The Southern states alone have thirty-five hundred such schools, many of them church run. These schools, of course, have enjoyed the tax-exempt status of other American religious and educational institutions.

Does the fact that a segregation academy is run by a church mean it does not have to abide by federal integration guidelines? Members of some Christian churches say that is just what it means. They claim the Bible forbids people of different races to mingle and live together, and that claim makes a belief in segregation part of their religious convictions. If government forces them to integrate — by ordering their schools to admit blacks or give up their tax exemptions, for instance — it is interfering in the free exercise of their religion. Whose right is greater — a school official's to practice segregation based on religious belief, or the government's to insist that boys and girls of all races get equal treatment?

Religion and government come into conflict in business and industry, too. Suppose a job applicant belongs to a faith that celebrates Saturday as a holy day. Can an employer refuse to hire someone who will not promise to work Saturdays? Should applicants have to give up their religious convictions to get a job? Or should the employer have to put up with the extra expense and inconvenience of accommodating an employee's religion? If employer and employee disagree, and one takes the other to court, which side will the court favor? How can government strike a balance between protecting the religious rights of workers and the economic interests of employers?

In some cases, a person may refuse, for religious reasons, to perform actions that most others take for granted. For example, Quakers and members of other pacifist groups will not fight for their country, citing their "conscientious objection" to warfare. Jehovah's Witnesses will neither go to war nor take part in any other aspect of public life (aside from paying their taxes). The refusal of Jehovah's Witnesses to allow their children to salute the flag in school led, in the 1930s and 1940s, to several court cases. The Witnesses claimed the First Amendment protected their refusal, and the government maintained that reciting the Pledge of Allegiance is a patriotic duty that schools have a right to demand.

Sometimes government has even been called upon to regulate the manner in which men and women may worship in their own churches or on their own property. That happened in the summer of 1979 in rural Pennsylvania, during a camp meeting of the Voice of the Nazarene Association of Independent Churches. Association members praise God with loud song and prayer, and at this particular meeting, they set up loud-speakers to amplify their worship. Non-Nazarene neighbors complained about the noise and asked local law officers to put an end to it. The neighbors had a legitimate grievance; the noise level was tremendous and had been for days. But the Nazarenes contended that enthusiastic singing and praying was required in their religion. "If we have to tone down our services, we might as well quit," one minister complained. Did the state have the right to make him quit just to preserve the peace?

Yes. That was the answer of local government in Pennsylvania.

A justice of the peace ruled that the Nazarenes were disturbing the peace and levied a fine against them. In his view, the issue centered on the loudspeakers. The group had every right to obey what it saw as the Biblical command to offer loud praise to God, the justice of the peace said. But the Bible says nothing about using an amplifying system, and it was that which turned lawful hymn singing into a public nuisance. Singing and praying are a legitimate part of the Nazarene's religious practices and thus protected under the First Amendment. Loudspeakers are not.

In effect, the justice of the peace was saying that although Americans may worship freely according to their beliefs, they do not have the right to impose those beliefs on other people. The First Amendment says every American is entitled to religious liberty, but it does not say that any one church or group is to enjoy special privileges denied to other groups, or to nonbelievers. With this in mind, let's go back and take a closer look at the questions we have raised in this chapter.

7. Special Privilege and the First Amendment

Jehovah's Witnesses cannot be made to salute the flag. In 1943, the Supreme Court reversed an earlier decision and ruled that school authorities have no right to compel students to make a public display of patriotism. "No official, high or petty," the Court said, "can prescribe what shall be orthodox in politics, nationalism, religion, or other matters of opinion." Similarly, the Court said, an individual may claim conscientious objector status and avoid military service as long as that individual acts out of sincere religious or moral conviction. Government cannot force anyone to act against his or her conscience.

In the world of business, the First Amendment is interpreted to mean that employers must make "reasonable accommodation" to workers' religious needs. The owner of a business may not routinely reject job applications from people who cannot work Saturdays, or whose beliefs keep them from doing a particular task. In a 1981 decision, the Supreme Court strengthened this position by upholding the right of a Jehovah's Witness to refuse to help in the manufacture of military equipment.

In fact, the Equal Employment Opportunity Commission of the federal government forbids employers even to ask applicants how their religion might affect their ability to do a job. The commission feels that permitting such a question could lead to widespread discrimination against some groups. But at the same time, workers may not "hinder" their employers by making impossible demands based on religious beliefs. For instance, nurses, air traffic controllers, and policemen cannot neglect their jobs in favor of performing religious rituals. Not only would such neglect inconvenience their employers, it could endanger the public.

In 1980 the commission issued written guidelines so employers and workers would understand their rights in regard to religious rules and time-off requirements. These guidelines are not absolute, however, and both workers and employers are likely to protest many of them. Some cases may end up in court and that will probably mean revised regulations in the future.

The amount of regulation government can impose on church-run schools and other institutions may change in the months and years ahead, too. In the past, the federal government has accepted the argument of hundreds of private schools that racial segregation can be defended under the First Amendment's free-exercise clause. Soon things may be different. A United States court has ordered an end to tax exemptions for Mississippi schools that cannot prove they are making an honest effort to attract and select black students and teachers. From now on, "segregation academies" in that state will find it more expensive to use "religious freedom" as a justification for breaking state and federal integration rulings. This court decision emphasized equal civil rights for blacks and whites over the right of a church to impose segregation on its community. But the decision applied only to Mississippi and it is uncertain whether it will be extended to other states.

In Texas, Lester Roloff closed down the Rebekah Home — temporarily. While it was closed, he reorganized it, making it a part of his church. Reopened in 1981, the school won the backing of a state judge, who ruled that under the separation clause of the First Amendment, a government cannot intervene in a church-owned and -operated institution.

The Texas ruling suggests that courts may eventually rule in favor of parochial schools that are suing for freedom from state education standards. By the early 1980s, such suits were pending in at least thirty states. Courts may even decide that parents like Thomas Hemple may keep their children out of school altogether. Of course, public-school officials and others will continue to argue that academic standards have nothing to do with freedom of religion.

Another 1981 court decision, this one in California, also endorsed the separation principle. California fundamentalists had brought suit to force public-school science teachers to instruct students in creationism as well as in the theory of evolution. The judge in this case ruled that teaching evolution, and evolution alone, does not violate the religious rights of those who believe in the literal truth of the Bible. He emphasized that California law already requires teachers to present the theory of evolution as just that — a theory — and to tell students that scientists do not agree on exactly how evolution takes place.

Court decisions on religious observances in public schools have also reinforced the separation of church and state. The 1980 Massachusetts prayer law was only six weeks old when the state's Supreme Judicial Court ruled it unconstitutional. The court said the law violated the antiestablishment clause of the Constitution. It gave special status to Christianity. The law discriminated against the public-school children of non-Christians by forcing them to either participate in a Christian ritual or be banished from the room. For the same reason, the U.S. Supreme Court overturned the Kentucky law requiring the Ten Commandments to be displayed in classrooms. Posting Bible selections, like engaging in Christian prayer, means favoring one religion over all others. Nevertheless, months after the court ruling in this case, many Kentucky school boards were still ordering that the Ten Commandments be displayed in public schools.

Court decisions that reinforce the separation of church and state have been welcomed not just by non-Christians but by Christians as well. To millions of devout Catholics and Protestants, the separation principle is more important than public displays of Christian devotion. They know that nothing in the Constitution, nor in any federal, state, or local law, prohibits private, personal devotion. How could it? As one church-owned newspaper, the *Christian Science Monitor,* pointed out editorially, "The nice thing about praying — in school or anywhere else — is that Congress or any other legislative body does not have to give anyone the 'right' to do it. It's an inherent right and privilege, granted by an authority much higher than any human legislative or judicial body."

The *Monitor* makes an excellent point, but even so, many Americans will go on trying to get special status for their conviction that all students should pray publicly and be exposed to religious ideas and values throughout each school day. Arkansas legislators have passed a law to require the teaching of Biblical creationism in every public school in the state. Other state legislatures and local school boards in other parts of the country are following suit.

Americans also continue to consider abortion and

birth control. After Congress and the states cut the use of public money for abortion, more than a hundred Protestant ministers and Jewish rabbis gathered in Washington, D.C., to protest the reductions. The clergymen wanted to "remind" Congress that it is the legal right of each woman — not of the government — to decide whether to have an abortion. They argued that drastically reducing public funding for abortion discriminates against the poor by denying them medical care available to middle- and upper-income women.

The clergymen also pointed out that by restricting abortion, legislators violate the antiestablishment clause of the First Amendment. Only a handful of America's many churches oppose abortion unless it is absolutely necessary to save a woman's life. Many groups support a woman's right to choose the operation under a wider variety of circumstances. A 1979 Gallup poll reveals that less than one fifth of Americans flatly oppose abortion. Thus, antiabortion laws force people of all religions to live by the doctrines of a few. "The state is obligated to ensure that all religions are respected equally before the law," the protesting clergymen said.

Many people feel that this argument also applies to contraception. If people do not want to use birth control because their religion forbids it, that is their right. But under the First Amendment, it is not their right to compel others to do the same.

Nevertheless, the religious convictions of those who oppose birth control seem to be guiding government policy today. Until recently, the federal government spent millions of dollars each year on family-planning programs. Much of the money went toward programs for teen-agers. But when Ronald Reagan became president, members of his administration declared their opposition to such programs and reduced funding for them. That may make birth control, like abortion, available to the rich but not to the poor. It also violates the First Amendment by transforming the religious position of a few churches into national policy.

The right-to-die issue will be coming in for public debate, too. Medical know-how has raced far ahead of lawmaking in this area. New medicines, improved techniques, and sophisticated mechanical equipment enable doctors to keep patients alive for weeks and months — even years — longer than they used to. In many cases, that means people can go on living happy and useful lives despite serious illnesses.

In cases like that of Brother Joseph Charles Fox, though, the results are less clear. Was Brother Fox really alive as he lay in that Long Island hospital? The people around him disagreed, and present-day law gives no real answer. We need new laws to deal with the rights of terminally ill patients, and with the rights of their relatives and doctors, too.

One possibility is to give legal status to so-called living wills. Living wills enable people to decide, while they are in good health, whether they want their lives prolonged by "extraordinary measures" in the event of a long-drawn-out terminal illness. They give individuals the opportunity to live — and die — according to their own moral and religious convictions, not someone else's.

A living will, however, would not permit the carrying out of a mercy killing. In 1981 a New York court backed up the idea behind living wills by ruling that a relative or legal guardian may order a terminally ill patient taken off life-support systems *if* the patient is mentally incompetent and *if* he has earlier expressed the wish to be allowed to die.

Ensuring society against mercy killings was also the concern of a presidential commission appointed in 1978 to study such ethical medical problems. In mid-1981, the commission recommended that all fifty states adopt laws that define death as the "irreversible cessation of all functions of the entire brain . . ."

After matters like the right to die and abortion, conflicts over a parent's right to withhold medicine from a sick child seem relatively simple to resolve. Hardly a court in the land would fail to order any treatment necessary to save life. (An exception is when the patient is badly handicapped or brain-damaged. In the Massachusetts case of the retarded leukemia victim, the courts allowed the guardian to stop treatment. Courts have ordered children to be given medicine and vaccinations over their parents' objections. They have ordered blood transfusions for the children of Jehovah's Witnesses, and dismissed lawsuits by Christian Scientists seeking to prevent fluoride, which medical evidence shows helps prevent tooth decay, from being added to public water supplies.

One judge summed up the American legal attitude toward conflicts between a child's welfare and the parents' right to exercise their religious beliefs:

"The right to practice religion freely does not include liberty to expose the community or the child to communicable disease or the latter to ill health or death . . . Parents may be free to become martyrs themselves. But it does not follow that they are free, in identical circumstances, to make martyrs of their children."

Actually, American law does not even allow all adults to become martyrs. Judges have ordered blood transfusions for some Jehovah's Witnesses who are of legal age. In a case involving members of the Mormon church, a justice of the Supreme Court said that a widow would not have the legal right to commit suicide, as once prescribed by Mormon law. In another case, the court upheld state laws against snake handling. Members of snake-handling sects believe their religious faith will protect them as they grasp these venomous creatures. But American courts hold that not even adults have an absolute right to endanger their own lives for religious reasons in all cases.

Finally, what happened in the case of the two Detroit men accused of the murder of Charles Williams, the Jehovah's Witness who died after refusing blood transfusions? Charges against one of the two were dropped. The man who fired the bullet that actually struck Williams, however, was charged with murder in the second degree — assault with intent to commit murder.

After a year's delay, the accused man, Timothy Marshall, went on trial. His defense was that Williams had died as a direct result of refusing transfusions and only as an *in*direct result of the shooting. Questioning the emergency room doctor, Marshall's lawyer elicited the opinion that Williams, but for his religious scruples, would "probably" have survived the shooting.

In the end, Timothy Marshall was convicted of careless and reckless use of a firearm. But he was acquitted of the more serious second-degree-murder charge.

According to his lawyer, Marshall will serve about three and a half years in jail — a punishment for what he did, not for another man's religious convictions.

8. A Question of Cults

The Disciples of Christ is a Protestant denomination with almost one and a half million members in the United States. The church, which has its national headquarters in Indianapolis, is loosely organized; each of its 4347 congregations is free to govern itself and arrange its worship services in its own way.

In 1965, the minister of one Disciples of Christ church in Indiana decided to leave the Midwest and head for California. Arriving in San Francisco, he established a new church, which he called the People's Temple.

This minister had great ambitions for his Temple and for the world. He believed that in time, mankind would achieve complete racial harmony and social justice. Looking forward to that time, he organized his church as a nonracist Christian-socialist group. Black and white lived and worked together in the People's Temple, sharing food and material goods in communal style.

Before long, the People's Temple was attracting

notice. News reporters wrote glowing stories about its social aims and accomplishments. California welfare authorities began placing homeless children in the Temple's care. The mayor of San Francisco appointed the minister head of the city housing commission and lesser members of the congregation were named to other government jobs. The group flourished and by the mid-1970s there were People's Temple communes as far away as Vancouver, British Columbia. Public compliments about the group's activities even came from the nation's vice president and its First Lady.

In 1978, the minister decided to move again, this time to the South American nation of Guyana. There, he and his thousand-odd followers established a town in the jungle wilderness. There, they built homes, a school, a library, and medical facilities. There, Temple members, including the California foster children, lived and worshiped together. And there, in November 1978, 911 members of the People's Temple committed mass suicide and murder, goaded into the grisly killings by the ravings of their leader, the Reverend Jim Jones.

Shock and horror swept the nation as Americans learned of the jungle massacre. Shock, horror, and a question: What about the country's other religious cults? Might they one day prove as deadly as the People's Temple?

The United States has many cults — as many as a thousand, according to an estimate in *U.S. News and*

World Report. The magazine also reports that up to
three million people — most of them in their teens and
twenties — belong to these cults.

One of the largest American cults is the Unification
Church, founded by the Reverend Sun Myung Moon.
About five thousand young Americans are full-time
members of this movement. The church's $10 million
annual income is raised partly through donations and
partly by church members who run businesses, beg for
handouts, and sell novelty items in the streets.

Unification Church members are not like the members of more conventional religious groups. They don't
just show up for services once or twice a week and live
and work with friends and family the rest of the time.
Instead, the Unification Church becomes their whole
life. "Moonies" drop out of school or quit their jobs,
leave home, and go to live at "training centers" with
other cult members. They give away their personal be-
longings and turn their money over to Moon. Most
break completely with family and friends.

Members of a Unification Church community have
little freedom of action. They are required to perform
whatever work their leader orders. They marry and
have children at his command. Cult members have no
freedom of thought, either. They must demonstrate
unquestioning faith in Moon's theology, which one
writer has described as "a mind-boggling mixture of

pentecostal Christianity, Eastern mysticism, anti-communism, pop psychology, and metaphysics."

According to Moon, God created Adam and Eve and placed them in the Garden of Eden to become the parents of a perfect race. They failed, as the book of Genesis tells us. Later, God sent Jesus to redeem mankind, but, says Moon, he died before fulfilling his mission. Now God is sending a new messiah to save the world. Although Moon does not actually say he himself is that messiah, he does admit that the messiah was born in 1920 in the east-central Asian nation of Korea. Moon, a native of South Korea, was born in 1920.

Naturally, people outside the Unification Church find all this controversial. Devout Christians and Jews see blasphemy in Moon's thinly veiled claim to be the messiah. Parents of Unification Church members see their families broken up, destroyed. "Our daughter is not our daughter anymore," said the mother of one college girl who became a Moonie in 1974. Parents don't like to see their children impoverish themselves by turning over all their possessions and money to the cult. They note that while cult members are practically paupers, Moon lives in a $750,000 mansion and is reported to have $13 million salted away in his private bank account.

People who live near Unification Church communities have other objections to the cult. They don't like the constant begging and the insistent sales pitches. Nor do they like it when Moonies begin to compete with local businesses. In the seacoast town of Gloucester, Massachusetts, Unification Church members set up a commercial fishery. The Moonies do not pay themselves salaries for their work, so long-time Gloucester fishermen fear the church members may begin to sell their catch at extra-low prices. That would hurt the local fishing industry.

The federal government has doubts of its own about Sun Myung Moon. Some people in Washington suspect that Moon's religious activities may be a front for political activities. They know for sure that one branch of the Unification Church, the Freedom Leadership Foundation, openly tries to persuade government officials to increase United States military and economic aid to South Korea. A few members of Congress are convinced that the church is closely linked to the South Korean Central Intelligence Agency, a link that could be illegal. It is a fact that two of Moon's personal aides were once colonels in the South Korean army.

The Unification Church's probable ties to a foreign nation make it unusual among religious cults. But in other ways the church is a typical cult, and criticisms of it are criticisms that are often made about other cults.

Moon is not the only cult leader who seeks to isolate converts and alienate them from their families. A former member of a Hare Krishna community in San Diego told reporters, "I always got along with my parents. I was real close to them. But they [the Hare Krishnas] told me that my parents were influenced by demons. That was very hard to take."

Separating cult members from their families is just one technique of the "brainwashing" that critics say is a common practice in cults. Others include depriving members of sleep, not giving them enough nourishing food, and making them sit through hours of exhausting religious rituals. Jim Jones used all these techniques on members of the People's Temple. The former Hare Krishna told reporters the effect such techniques can have: "They wake you up at 4:00 A.M. and you start chanting over and over. You're not really there, you're so tired. They pile on the spiritual answers but you don't have enough time to think about whether they make sense."

Once the cult leader has gained a kind of "mind control" over a convert, he can be confident that his every order will be carried out. "Every activity you do is what they tell you to do," the Hare Krishna explained. It's the same for Moonies and other cultists, the critics say. Certainly it was that way for the 911 men, women, and children who followed Jim Jones's order to destroy themselves and each other in Guyana.

That's how it is for members of many cults. Charles Dederich, leader of a religious cult known as Synanon, says, "I am not bound by the rules. I make them." Dederich tells his followers when to have children and when not to, and they obey him. When he gave up smoking, he forced his eighteen hundred disciples to give it up, too. When his wife went on a diet, so did everyone else in Synanon.

Eventually, a charismatic cult leader may gain so much control over his people that he, and they, come to believe he is no longer God's mouthpiece, but God himself. Jim Jones staged fake miracles to impress his flock and claimed he could raise the dead. Apparently he was believed. Sun Myung Moon delivers broad hints about the identity of the new messiah. George Baker, founder of a cult that won thousands of converts among America's black population fifty years ago, called himself Father Divine. No wonder blasphemy is a charge leveled at many a cult leader.

Another way in which the Unification Church is typical is that its leader surrounds himself with worldly luxury while his followers labor and donate money to support him. Moon is rich; Moonies are poor. Similarly, Charles Dederich's annual income is $100,000, but ordinary Synanon members pay $400 a month to live in one of the group's communities. One woman has given the church $1 million.

The same is true of the Church of Scientology, founded in 1955 by a man named L. Ron Hubbard. Hubbard began his career in the 1940s as a writer of science fiction, but even then he dreamed of a better life. "Writing for a penny a word is ridiculous," he once told a friend. "If a man really wanted to make a million dollars, the best way would be to start his own religion." Hubbard has done both. So has the head of the Worldwide Church of God, Herbert W. Armstrong. Radio and television appeals have brought millions upon millions of dollars into church headquarters in Pasadena, California. Armstrong and his top aides live and travel in high style, staying in the world's finest hotels, frequenting night clubs, decorating their homes extravagantly, and concluding real-estate deals worth hundreds of thousands of dollars.

Cult members accept their leaders' luxurious lives as wholeheartedly as they accept their religious teachings and day-by-day commands. "Why must a religious leader be an ascetic?" one Moonie wanted to know. After all, he might have added, the Catholic church and other churches, too, possess vast wealth.

Creating a public nuisance is another charge made against the Unification Church and other cults. Street begging and selling can be a nuisance, and so can cultists' determined efforts to win new converts. In some cities, people are hardly able to walk down the street without being buttonholed by eager young proselytizers. This worries parents who fear their children, too, will fall under the influence of a cult.

Some cult leaders progress from creating a nuisance

to committing crimes. Charles Dederich struck back at one attorney who brought a lawsuit against Synanon by having a rattlesnake placed in his mailbox. The attorney was bitten, though not fatally. In another case, five members of the Church of Scientology, including Mrs. L. Ron Hubbard, were convicted of breaking into government offices in order to steal records relating to their cult.

The pattern of abuse in religious cults seems clear. Crime, creating a nuisance, greed, blasphemy, despotic control over people's minds and lives — all are part of the picture. Many Americans knew that long before they ever heard of Jim Jones. But after the Guyana killings, thousands of people began asking if something could — or should — be done to control cult activities. To find out, Senator Robert Dole of Kansas opened informal congressional hearings on the subject.

The hearings lasted only four hours. It took no more time than that to demonstrate that anticult laws are impossible under the U.S. Constitution.

Not that some witnesses at the hearing didn't have suggestions for legislation. Richard Delgado, professor of law at the University of Washington, proposed laws to force street proselytizers to identify themselves and their organizations clearly. It has been the practice of cultists to talk to possible converts in very general terms about "feeling dissatisfied" or "wanting a purpose in life." Only when converts are actually in cult headquarters, cut off from their families and mentally and physically exhausted by religious brainwashing, may they realize they have committed themselves to a cult.

Delgado had other suggestions. Proselytizers could be required to apply for government licenses. Would-be converts might have to wait through a "cooling-off" period before formally joining a cult. Finally, new laws could allow the courts to force converts to undergo psychiatric treatment aimed at getting them to renounce the cult. This treatment would resemble the "deprogramming" that the families of some cult members have turned to in an attempt to overcome the effects of cult brainwashing upon their children. Cult members who are deprogrammed may be forcibly abducted, locked up, and made to listen to hours upon hours of questions and statements that challenge cult teachings. Deprogramming is highly controversial. One professional deprogrammer has been sentenced to jail for his activities, which many see as violating the religious freedom of cultists. Yet at Senator Dole's hearing, people were suggesting that Congress make deprogramming mandatory in some cases.

What would be wrong with laws like these? The first problem: deciding which groups to apply them to. What is a cult, anyway?

Webster's dictionary defines *cult* as a system of worship of a deity; the rites of a religion; or great devotion to some person, idea, or thing. The same dictionary says *religion* is the service and adoration of God or a god; a system of faith and worship; an awareness or conviction of the existence of a supreme being, arousing reverence, love, gratitude, the will to serve and obey.

What, based on those definitions, is the difference between a cult and a religion?

People have tried to come up with answers. A genuine religious group is large, they say, like this country's forty-nine-million-member Catholic church, or its Lutheran churches, with their ten million members. Cults, by contrast, are small, claiming at most a few thousand devotees.

That is not a very valid distinction. Abraham, the father of Judaism, set forth for the Promised Land with his wife, his nephew, and a handful of followers. Christianity began with Jesus and his twelve disciples. Obviously, the size of a religious group has little to do with its quality.

Well, then, people say, you can tell a cult from a real religion because cultists go in for bizarre beliefs and actions. Hare Krishnas shave their heads, wear long robes, and chant in the streets. Moonies reject their middle-class values and go begging. Members of the cult of Wicca practice witchcraft.

Yet most people accept Christian Science as a "real" religion — and what could be odder than for intelligent, loving parents to allow a child to die of pneumonia for lack of ordinary penicillin? Mormons are respected as sober, industrious, law-abiding citizens, but a century ago, Mormons practiced polygamy out of religious conviction. Even today, a few Mormon men have more than one wife, although the Mormon church has officially condemned polygamy since the end of the nineteenth century. Jews and Protestants find it hard to accept that Catholics believe bread and wine turn into the body and blood of Jesus during the sacrament of communion. Christians wonder at the Orthodox Jewish prohibition against eating meat and milk together — or even eating them at different times from the same dishes. Every religion has beliefs or rituals that people outside the faith find unusual. Oddity is no standard for identifying cults.

What about the test of time? Mormonism, Christian Science, and Judaism have been around for years. The Unification Church and Scientology have not. Perhaps longevity is the way to distinguish between a religion and a cult.

But a Christian will tell you that the teachings of Jesus were as valid in A.D. 33 as they are today. And a Moonie will answer that since Sun Myung Moon is the *new* messiah, 1982 is the same for the Unification Church as A.D. 33 was for the Christian. Of course, the Moonie may not believe that ten or twenty years from now. By then the Unification Church may no longer exist. But that doesn't settle the question for right now. In a few decades, Moon's church could be one of the world's major religions. Is it a cult or isn't it?

Even if we should decide that the Unification Church and certain other groups were cults, the government would have trouble using anticult laws against them. Suppose Congress did pass legislation requiring members of specified religious groups to obtain licenses to proselytize. It's a safe bet that someone would violate the law. Sooner or later, an unlicensed missionary would be arrested and brought to trial.

Almost any judge would throw the case out of court on the grounds that the licensing law was a triple violation of the First Amendment. Such a law would limit a cultist's freedom of speech. It would also take away his freedom to practice his religion, since many cults require their members to seek converts. In addition, by discriminating against so-called cults, the law would make an establishment of those religions whose active members do not have to be licensed. Other anticult laws along the lines of those suggested by Professor Delgado would surely get similar treatment in court.

Still, it must be possible to do something to control cults, especially cults as deadly as the People's Temple turned out to be. After the Guyana killings, some Americans criticized the Federal Bureau of Investigation for failing to heed rumors that Jones was insane, heavily armed, and a menace to those around him.

They said the FBI ought to have infiltrated the Temple in San Francisco and gathered hard evidence of illegal activities there. Yet if the FBI had become involved, one agent scoffed, "Can't you just hear the roar?"

The roar would have been tremendous if the FBI had been caught trying to spy on the cult, of course. But California social workers would have been within their rights to have looked more carefully into the cult before placing foster children there.

There are laws that can be applied to religious groups without infringing on their liberties. Health and sanitary codes are enforced for schools, businesses, restaurants, libraries — just about anywhere people congregate. They apply to churches, too, and can be especially helpful in safeguarding those who live in cult communities, where conditions are often overcrowded.

Police agencies could have looked into the charge that the People's Temple was accumulating illegal weapons. Guns can be dangerous whether they are handled by Catholics, Protestants, Jews, members of the People's Temple, atheists, or self-styled witches. It is not a violation of the First Amendment to require religious groups — all religious groups — to obey the law of the land.

Laws that require parochial schools to meet state education standards are valid, and can be used to help protect children and young adults from cultists' brainwashing techniques. Tax-exemption laws should be the same for all religions. As we have seen, the federal government has fought exemptions for such church-owned businesses as the Christian Brothers winery. It is not discriminatory for it to oppose exemptions for money-making activities by cults.

Laws to protect people's civil rights can also be equally enforced. A North Carolina minister, head of the Church of God and True Holiness, and two of his followers are now in federal prisons, convicted on charges of keeping other church members in slavery, beating them, and forcing them to work at menial jobs. The three were tried under antislavery laws. That's hardly discriminatory. No religious institution in the country can be permitted to enforce slave labor. Nor can any church leader be permitted to mete out "cruel and unusual punishment" the way Jim Jones did and others have. Cruel and unusual punishment is unconstitutional under the Eighth Amendment.

But although applying laws already on the books to cults and other religious groups may not be discriminatory, it won't be easy, either. That is because whenever government tries to regulate the activities of even one small sect, it runs into the united opposition of nearly all of America's largest and most influential religious groups.

In 1979, the attorney general of the state of California began an investigation into the possible misuse or theft of funds from the Worldwide Church of God by the group's founder, Herbert Armstrong. The attorney general asked a California court to appoint someone outside the church to take over temporary control of its financial affairs. The court did so.

Armstrong fought the court action vigorously. In full-page ads in newspapers around the country, he demanded:

"Can you imagine the attorney general overseeing the spending of the Roman Catholic Church in California?

"Would he have attacked the Methodist Church, the Presbyterian or Lutheran?

"Would he have undertaken to raid a synagogue?

"*Will he?*"

Armstrong's implication was clear. If government acts against one sect, it can act against any.

Clergymen of many faiths thought Armstrong's point was well taken. The Catholic Church and several Protestant groups, including the National Council of Churches, filed legal briefs in behalf of the Worldwide Church of God and against the California court's action.

The publicity that resulted from the legal action may well have helped Armstrong's cause. In 1980, California passed a law making it impossible for state authorities to investigate church finances except in obviously criminal cases.

Six months later, three hundred representatives of

ninety of America's organized religions gathered in the nation's capital for a three-day conference. They were there to discuss church-state relations and the role government plays in regulating religious activity.

The delegates talked about tax exemptions for religious organizations, and about government efforts to limit some of those exemptions. They examined state and federal regulations on health and safety, education, and employment, and they wondered what effect they might have on churches. Over and over, the delegates asked each other, "Does government regulation threaten religious freedom in the United States today?"

The conferees could not agree on an answer. One Presbyterian representative said he did not believe that any one single regulatory action poses a danger. "But," he added, "the pattern that they form when viewed together is an alarming one, and that is why we are here."

Other speakers acknowledged that government must act to protect public health and safety. A Methodist minister concluded that in the light of what happened at the People's Temple in Guyana, he could justify "some kind of intervention." But it was a professor of law from Fordham University, a Catholic college in New York, who summed it up best. "There is no evidence of any concerted attack on the church," he declared. "But the government has posed certain enigmas for us."

The government has. At the same time, churches, with all their diverse beliefs and rituals, pose enigmas for government.

When, if ever, is government interference in religion justified? The California state government had to back off its investigation into the Worldwide Church of God. More recently, a federal grand jury began looking into charges of financial misdoings by John Cardinal Cody, the Roman Catholic Archbishop of Chicago. Should that investigation have been allowed? Late in 1981, the United States government charged the Reverend Sun Myung Moon with tax evasion. Was the charge legitimate — or just a way of "getting at" an unorthodox cult leader?

Can government intervention in religion ever be justified? Perhaps not. Shady financial doings — even the tragedy of a Jim Jones — may be the price we must pay for our religious liberty.

No one — not the wisest statesman nor the most devout ecclesiastic — can tell for sure.

9. Religious Rights Versus the Religious Right

Twice in American history a wave of Christian revivalism has swept the country. In the 1730s, a young Massachusetts minister named Jonathan Edwards began preaching a fiery brand of Calvinism, exhorting his listeners to abandon their sinful ways and return to the paths of righteousness. There followed the Great Awakening, during which thousands of New England men and women rededicated themselves to God and Christ. Before long, the revival spirit reached into the Middle Atlantic and Southern colonies. The Great Awakening lasted well into the 1760s.

Nearly a century later, America underwent another religious revival. This Second Awakening was led by Charles G. Finney, a Presbyterian minister who later turned to Congregationalism. Finney preached in New York City and, after becoming president of Oberlin College, in Ohio. He also made several trips to England. Wherever he spoke, people listened, and again, Americans experienced a spiritual renewal.

Now another revival is under way. It seems possible

that the 1980s will go down in history as the time of America's third great awakening.

In part, the new revival is a reaction to years of declining interest in religious and spiritual matters. In 1960, 64 percent of all Americans were church members. By 1977, that figure had dropped to 61 percent. But even more, the revival is a response to changes in American society.

Many of the changes have been in the home, within the family. A century ago, a man was the undisputed head of his household; his wife generally obeyed his bidding. Few women worked outside the home and only a tiny number had any professional training or advanced education. Divorce was rare and it was illegal for a woman to have an abortion.

Men were masters of their children, too, and most boys and girls were as obedient as their mothers. Young men often worked for their fathers, on the farm or in the family business, long after they reached adulthood.

Things are different today. Millions of teen-agers have weekend or after-school jobs. Many can afford to travel, own cars, or educate themselves. Women have entered the working world of business and factory and are more and more prominent in the professions. A woman can obtain an abortion without her husband's knowledge or divorce him against his will.

Other changes have occurred in society at large.

Once, white people owned blacks as slaves, and even after slavery was abolished, blacks continued to be treated as second-class citizens. Millions of blacks were denied a good education, decent homes, well-paying jobs, and the opportunity to mingle with whites, as well as being kept from voting and holding office. Even today, blacks and members of other minority groups may face unfair and unequal treatment. But laws passed in the 1960s and 1970s do seek to guarantee them the right to vote, use public facilities, go to college, and get good jobs.

Social programs are another change. Fifty years ago, state and federal governments did little to help the country's elderly, sick, and needy. Now governments do more, helping to provide food, clothing, shelter, medicine, jobs, and education to people who could not otherwise afford these things. With prices going up and jobs becoming hard to find, social service programs are important to millions of Americans.

Other changes involve the law. Courts are more careful than they used to be to guard the rights of people accused of crimes. In 1972, the Supreme Court threw out state death-penalty laws, declaring them unfair and unconstitutional. (Since then, though, several states have passed new laws that are acceptable under the Constitution to require capital punishment for certain crimes.)

America's relations with other nations have changed

too. Only a short time ago, most Americans thought of communist nations like the Soviet Union and the People's Republic of China as deadly and implacable enemies. Today, presidents welcome Chinese and Soviet leaders to the White House. Through the United Nations and other international agencies, the United States reaches out to communist and noncommunist nations alike with cultural exchanges, foreign aid, and trade arrangements.

Changes like these seem to be due to many different factors. Improved transportation and communications have brought nations closer together, and modern weapons, including nuclear weapons, make many countries eager to avoid war. Through books, newspapers, radio, and television, Americans know that miscarriages of justice can occur under the best of laws, and many are more alert to the need to protect the rights of the accused. News reporting has made apparent the injustice of racial segregation. It has shown what it is like to live in poverty and given millions of affluent Americans a sense of responsibility toward the less fortunate. Within families, economic pressures, such as the pressure of inflation, are forcing more and more women to work outside the home.

Economics, news coverage, social awareness, modern technology — all these and more seem to have helped bring about change in our society.

Or have they?

Millions of people would answer that question with a vehement *no*. According to them, our society has changed as we Americans have turned away from God. The changes — and the problems that accompany some of them — are signs of God's anger.

Take the changes within families. When women obeyed their husbands in all things, they, and their husbands, felt they were obeying God. "Women, submit yourselves unto your own husbands, as unto the Lord," St. Paul wrote in his letter to the Ephesians, one of the books of the New Testament. Similarly, the Old Testament instructs children to obey their parents. "Honor thy father and thy mother," says the Fifth Commandment.

But Americans have rejected the word of God. Wives and children no longer submit and obey, and the results, many believe, are plain to see. Divorce. Adultery. Teen-age runaways. Drug abuse. Unmarried mothers. Abortion.

In the same way, some think the Bible orders racial segregation. To them, a dark skin is the mark of Cain, the murderer. When God set Cain apart from other men, he established segregation. The push toward integration, which is contrary to the will of God, has helped bring about agitation for civil rights, "forced" busing, and occasional big-city rioting, they say.

Several passages in the Bible demand harsh punishments for lawbreakers. "Eye for eye, tooth for tooth, hand for hand, foot for foot," God told Moses, but we reject such ideas of retribution. The result? Convicted criminals, some free on parole, others because of legal technicalities or crowded court calendars, roam the streets. The violent-crime rate is rising.

Nor does the Bible condone government assistance to the needy. God put man on this earth to labor and support himself and his family by the sweat of his face. Many contend that social service programs thwart God's plan by encouraging people to sit around and let the government provide for their needs.

What of our relations with communist nations? Most communist governments discourage religion or try to suppress it altogether. Many believe the United States should shun "godless communism" and thereby set an example of righteousness, morality, and the fear of God.

What *has* caused the changes — and the problems — in our society? Are they a punishment from God? Or are they due to forces like economics and material progress?

Religious leaders, politicians, social scientists, writers, and others may debate such questions, but while they talk, others react. One reaction is the new spirit of revivalism evident around the country.

Signs of the revival are everywhere. Eighty million Americans consider themselves "evangelicals," who have been "born again" in Christ. Elected politicians, from U.S. presidents to local school board members, emphasize their faith and their reliance upon divine guidance. Churches are enlarging their facilities to provide more space for worship services and Sunday-school activities. In 1981, Christian schools were opening at the rate of three a day and some Jewish schools were increasing enrollments, too. Church attendance is up, just as it was in the days of Jonathan Edwards and Charles Finney.

Other signs of the revival are more typically twentieth-century. Religious slogans — "Honk If You Love Jesus" and "Smile, God Loves You" — adorn automobile bumpers. Sales of religious medals and other symbols are booming. Above all, there is the huge growth of electronic evangelism, the spreading of the Christian gospel via radio and television.

Electronic evangelism is the tool used by some two thousand American preachers to call sinners to repentance. It's a tool that works. By one estimate, 114 million Americans listen to radio preachers each week. (This estimate comes from religious broadcasters themselves, and many believe it is exaggerated.) Thirteen hundred radio stations, one out of every seven commercial stations in the country, is a "Christian" station. In addition, gospel hours are aired on stations that are not officially "Christian."

Television is essential to electronic evangelism. The Christian Broadcasting Network, founded by the Reverend Pat Robertson, owns a satellite transmitter that beams religious programming to 4 of its own channels and to 150 other stations. Another evangelist, the Reverend Jerry Falwell, claims to reach eighteen million Americans each week over 379 television and 400 radio stations. When Oral Roberts, an Oklahoma-based preacher, goes on television with one of his religious variety specials, he can count on upward of sixty million viewers.

Electronic evangelists, backed up by huge choirs, lavish sets, and elaborate stage effects, are adept at winning converts. They are skilled at raising money, too. Contributions from viewers of Oral Roberts's programs have enabled him to build a $150 million university and a $100 million medical center in Tulsa. Jerry Falwell raises $1 million a week, and Bill Bright, head of the Campus Crusade for Christ, takes in twice that. Pat Robertson's Christian Broadcasting Network raises millions annually. It has to, just to cover its operating expenses of $20 million a year.

Many Americans, including a lot of sincere Christians, feel that electronic evangelism puts too much emphasis on fund raising and relies too heavily on the techniques of show business and the advertising industry. Another aspect of the new revival disturbs them even more. That aspect has been dubbed the "religious right."

The name describes the movement well. It is reli-

gious, made up almost entirely of fundamentalist born-
again Protestants. It is also "right-wing," or conservative, in its social and political views. It is strongly
opposed to liberal or "left-wing" ideas.

One leader of the religious right is Jerry Falwell. Be-
sides preaching on radio and television, Falwell is the
minister of a seventeen-thousand-member Baptist
church in Lynchburg, Virginia. In June 1979 Falwell
organized the Moral Majority, a nationwide group of
72,000 fundamentalist clergymen. Another prominent
member of the religious right is Richard Zone, founder
of the two-thousand-member Christian Voice. Evangelists Pat Robertson, James Robison, and Jim Bakker
are also active in the movement.

The message Americans hear from Falwell and the
others is simple. America has turned away from God.
Our society has changed — for the worse. Controver-
sies over abortion, crime, welfare, and so on are a result of God's judgment upon a sinful nation. The
problems in our society exist because God is punishing
America for its iniquities.

"We must turn from our wicked ways!" thunders
James Robison. "If America does not go to her knees,
she'll go to her grave," warns a Chicago evangelist, Del
Fehsenfeld. Jerry Falwell concurs. "The future of the
nation is in your hands and mine," he told his fellow
ministers in Dallas, Texas, at a 1980 convention of
evangelists there.

The religious right seeks to replace American law with God's law as they believe that law is laid down in the Bible. "The Bible is God's rule book," says evangelist Howard Phillips. Accordingly, the religious right is pressing for one new constitutional amendment against abortion, which it believes the Bible condemns, and another new one to require school prayer, which it says the Bible demands. At the same time the Moral Majority and other groups are working to defeat the proposed constitutional Equal Rights Amendment (ERA), which would guarantee women the same civil and political rights men enjoy. In the evangelists' view, the Bible orders women to serve men, not act as their equals. The religious right wants to see an end to sex-education courses and government programs to provide birth-control information to women. It wants new laws to outlaw homosexuality and to keep homosexuals from working at certain jobs.

The leaders of the religious right also accuse courts of "coddling" criminals and they want to institute new, stricter legal proceedings based on Old Testament law. They want to cut back on the legal rights of minors and on the First Amendment guarantee of freedom of speech and the press. They want a federal death penalty for murder, rape, kidnaping, and treason. One fundamentalist minister has even called for the capital punishment of homosexuals.

The religious right opposes government social service

programs and its leaders demand an end to much of the public aid that millions of Americans need. They believe God gave the earth to man so man could have dominion over nature and use it as he wished. From this they conclude that present-day government regulation of business and industry — including rules aimed at preserving the environment — is wrong. They also maintain that the Bible commands government leaders to keep public budgets balanced, to make sure government spends no more money than it raises through taxes. As a matter of fact, the United States budget has only been balanced in one year since 1964, and it was sometimes unbalanced before that. In the first year of George Washington's administration, for example, federal expenses outran receipts by $60,000. Now that must stop, says the religious right, because God demands it. "We can talk about a balanced budget as a moral issue because the Bible says 'you should not live in debt,' " says Richard Zone.

God is displeased with what the United States is doing on the international scene, too, says the religious right. According to its interpretation of the Bible, God wants America to get tough with "godless" communist countries. "Giving in to the Soviet Union is not compatible with the Judeo-Christian heritage told in the Bible," one speaker told the evangelists at the 1980 Dallas convention. Instead of "giving in," as the religious right believes we have been doing, the United

States should build up its arsenals of nuclear and non-nuclear weapons and prepare for war.

The leaders of the religious right know what they want for America. What's more, they believe they have found the way to get it. Their plan is to fill the nation's political offices with people who completely share their point of view. In the late 1970s, conservative religious groups began a campaign to turn the nation's liberal senators, representatives, governors, state legislators, and mayors out of office and to replace them with political and religious conservatives. This campaign has been remarkably effective, as the 1980 election demonstrated.

The religious right began by "targeting" a number of politicians it wanted to see thrown out of office. Some were targeted because they favored government funding for abortions, others because they opposed school prayer or expressed support for the Equal Rights Amendment or for a federal department of education. Men like Falwell made it clear that if a politician opposed the religious right's position on *only one issue,* that politician was nonetheless marked for defeat. As an aide to one targeted senator, Frank Church of Idaho, pointed out, the religious right assumes that "if you're not 100 percent for them, you must be 100 percent against them."

Armed with its hit list, the religious right went to work. Many of the nation's electronic evangelists came on the air week after week to remind listeners that God is angry at America and that only if the country turns to Jesus Christ and the Bible will Americans be happy and prosperous again. Regulations of the federal government forbid the leaders of tax-exempt religious organizations to endorse candidates on the air, but the crusading evangelists manage to get around that restriction. Groups like the Moral Majority are divided into separate branches, one for education, another for legal action on religious issues, a third to promote government support for fundamentalist views, and a fourth to endorse political candidates. Falwell can condemn America's "immorality" from the pulpit on Sunday and then let the political arm of the Moral Majority endorse "morally sound" candidates at political gatherings during the rest of the week. Government regulations against churches becoming involved in politics don't apply to endorsements made in this way.

The national leadership of the religious right found plenty of support for its campaign against liberalism. Around the country, thousands of ministers, and some priests and a few rabbis, too, did their part to promote the conservative cause. Falwell offered Moral Majority members advice on how to influence lawmaking. "Here's what you do," he told Florida clergymen opposed to the Equal Rights Amendment. "You tell everybody in your congregation to bring two stamped envelopes to church on Sunday. You show them a couple of sample letters." The samples would express opposition to the ERA and threaten state politicians with defeat at the polls if they supported it. Falwell continued: "Make them write those letters in church . . . Do it right during the service."

Falwell had other suggestions for ministers. "You can register people to vote," he said. "You can explain the issues to them. And you can endorse candidates, right there in church on Sunday morning."

All this, the religious right did in 1980. The Moral Majority alone claims credit for registering four million new conservative voters before the 1980 election. It spent $3 million on just six races for the United States Senate. Besides that, the Moral Majority and similar right-wing religious organizations were involved in hundreds of other elections on every level of government.

Their efforts paid off. The presidential candidate favored by the religious right, conservative Republican Ronald Reagan, soundly defeated Democrat Jimmy Carter. Frank Church, targeted by the Moral Majority in Idaho, lost his seat in Congress. So did liberal senators and representatives in other states. Conservative governors and mayors replaced liberal ones in many places, and the political balance of several state houses also shifted to the right.

Immediately after the election, the religious right got to work planning for future victories. On November 10,

1980, Jerry Falwell spoke at a religious-political rally on the steps of the New Jersey state capitol. There he offered advice to New Jersey lawmakers. Officeholders, Falwell said, "would do well to examine their records and get in step with conservative values or be prepared to be unemployed."

The religious right hopes to affect other aspects of our lives. One of its goals is to eliminate what it considers pornography in books and magazines as well as on television and in the movies.

Religious groups in many parts of the country are urging people to avoid X- and R-rated movies, and to stop buying products advertised on television shows they think objectionable. This boycott strategy has worked before in television and it may well work again. In June 1981, Procter & Gamble, the household products company that is television's biggest advertiser, announced it was withdrawing its commercials from fifty programs deemed offensive by the religious right. When network executives announced their new programs for the fall of 1981, observers noted a swing away from the sexually suggestive material that was so popular in previous seasons.

The religious right believes in censoring books, too. The American Library Association reports that in the month after the 1980 election, efforts to ban library books increased 500 percent. Censorship requests involved works by such individuals as John Steinbeck,

Philip Roth, Judy Blume, and William Shakespeare. In one case, a religious group succeeded in removing from library shelves a volume called *Making It with Mademoiselle*. Obviously, the censors had not bothered to look at the book; it contained sewing instructions compiled by the staff of *Mademoiselle* magazine!

In some places, members of the religious right demand that librarians publicize the names of borrowers of "objectionable" books and materials. A Washington state branch of the Moral Majority went to court to try to force the state library to disclose the identities of schools that had used a library film on sex education. Many Americans find the idea of any church or religious organization — or any organization for that matter — checking up on Americans' reading and viewing habits terrifying. But checking up is exactly what the religious right is doing.

Does the religious right threaten American liberties? Consider the words of one conservative minister, Ben Patterson of California. "Why go through the inconvenience of having to live with diversity when you can organize your own group, and perhaps use the instruments of power to impose the will of your group on everyone else?" he wrote.

The religious right threatens American liberties, not because it wants moral standards, but because it claims that only one set of standards, its own, is acceptable to God. The religious right would compel every person in the country to abide by its definitions of right and wrong. Its leaders have said publicly that God will not tolerate even the smallest deviation from their fundamentalist morality. Only when Americans cast off their false values will God smile upon the nation again.

Sound familiar? It should. The religious right echoes John Calvin's dictum of four hundred years ago: "The punishments executed upon false prophets, and seducing teachers, do bring down the showers of God's blessings upon the civil state."

Like Calvin, and like many of America's early colonists, the leaders of the religious right believe in theocratic government. They want to see a perfect union between church and state. They are trying to bring about the precise opposite of what the writers of the Constitution planned for the country.

The church-state envisioned by the religious right would be unconstitutional on several grounds, say its critics. Insistence on religious conformity among elected officials defies Article VI of the Constitution, which prohibits any religious test for office. Turning fundamentalist religious belief into law would violate the First Amendment's antiestablishment clause. And if religious intolerance toward nonfundamentalists grows, the free exercise of religion could be limited in the United States.

The religious right denies that its aims are unconstitutional. Its leaders say they are tolerant of other religions, pointing out that some members of both Christian and non-Christian faiths agree with them on some issues.

Nor do they believe that putting their moral standards into law would amount to an establishment of religion. After all, laws are *supposed* to incorporate moral standards. America, like every other nation, has laws against murder. Why not laws against abortion, too, since many consider abortion a form of killing? The religious right also reminds its critics that American religious leaders have always been involved in politics. Charles Finney, for instance, abhorred America's system of slavery, and the Second Awakening helped bring about the antislavery abolitionist movement. During the 1950s, 1960s and 1970s, members of the clergy were active in the drive for civil rights, and many worked for an end to American fighting in the war in Vietnam. Many times religious groups have had a decisive influence on elections, lawmaking, and public policy.

As for the charge that the religious right seeks to impose religious tests for office, that is silly, its leaders say. Naturally voters are going to examine a candidate's positions before casting their ballots. That is their right, and their duty, as responsible citizens of a democracy.

It is not that simple, critics of the religious right respond. Clergymen of the religious right don't just inform church members about political issues. They tell them exactly where God wants them to stand on each issue, and turn church services into political action meetings. They don't just say they think one candidate is better than another; they label candidates they oppose "wicked" or "sinful." According to Representative Michael L. Synar of Oklahoma, some leaders of the religious right actually conspire to set up liberal politicians ahead of time so they will be sure to fail religious tests for office when the next election comes around.

For example, Synar says, before the 1980 election, the Moral Majority and other groups got sympathetic members of Congress to submit proposals for extremely conservative new laws — proposals they knew had no chance of passing. Congressman Synar, like many congressional liberals and moderates, voted against the proposals. The Moral Majority's political action branch recorded how each senator and representative voted in each case. Months later, the records were used against targeted candidates.

Such long-term, highly organized tactics by religious groups are new to American politics. Church-related civil rights and antiwar organizations did not set up legislators in order to have political ammunition to use against them at a later date. More similar to the religious right's tactics were some of the anti-Catholic campaigns of the past, especially those employed in the

1928 and 1960 elections. But even the radical anti-Catholics of a few decades ago lacked the present-day religious right's advantage of sophisticated advertising techniques, electronic fund raising, coast-to-coast broadcasting networks, and computerized mailing lists.

The critics also maintain that by working for laws that embody its specific moral positions, the religious right truly does threaten to establish itself as an official religion. Laws against murder cannot be equated with laws against abortion, they say. Nearly all people in all times and places have agreed that murder is wrong, but there is no such general agreement on abortion. Still less do people agree on the morality or immorality of birth control, divorce, homosexuality, environmentalism, welfare, or the economics of communism.

Critics also question the religious right's contention that it respects the beliefs of other faiths. Instead of respect, they see signs of prejudice and bigotry.

At the 1980 Dallas convention of fundamentalists, Dr. Bailey Smith, president of the Southern Baptist Convention, spoke to his fellow evangelists about religious observances at political events. "It is interesting," Smith mused, "at great political rallies how you have a Protestant to pray, a Catholic to pray, and then you have a Jew to pray. With all due respect . . . my friends, God Almighty does not hear the prayer of a Jew."

So much for Jews. If God doesn't hear them, why

should they bother to pray? If Jews aren't going to pray, why should they have synagogues? It's not a very big step from "God does not hear the prayer of a Jew" to "Let's not let Jews pray," as many Jewish survivors of the time of the Nazi Holocaust will testify.

About a month after he made that statement, Smith denied that he was anti-Semitic. As he explained it, "I am pro-Jew . . . but without Jesus Christ they are lost. No prayer gets through that is not prayed through Jesus Christ." Later, in a broadcast sermon, Smith remarked to a national audience, "Jews have funny-looking noses." Again, an explanation was forthcoming; Smith said he was joking. He may have been, but few Jews were laughing. They knew Smith is not the only fundamentalist who has made anti-Jewish remarks. And they know that nationwide, anti-Semitic attacks increased threefold between 1979 and 1980.

Jews are not the only ones who may run into prejudice from the religious right. At a recent Bible conference organized by James Robison, fundamentalist Dr. Curtis Hutson was scheduled to share a platform with Phyllis Schlafly. Schlafly, a religious and political conservative, opposes the Equal Rights Amendment and has campaigned against it around the country. Hutson is also against the ERA, and he and Schlafly agree on other issues. But Schlafly is a Catholic, and when Hutson learned that he was to appear with her, he withdrew from the conference. "I cannot speak at a Bible conference with a Roman Catholic lady," he announced.

Catholics . . . Jews . . . who else might experience intolerance from the religious right? Unitarians who deny the Trinity? Episcopalians who believe in evolution? Congregationalists who do not think every word in the Bible is to be taken literally? Fundamentalists with liberal political ideas?

It could happen. And there are fundamentalists, along with Congregationalists, Episcopalians, Unitarians, and others, who are very much aware of that fact. In fact, some of the most outspoken critics of the religious right are born-again Christians. They welcome the religious revival spirit of the 1980s in general, but they worry about the growing influence of the religious right upon that revival.

Some are dismayed by the religious right's preoccupation with military affairs. One participant at the 1980 Dallas convention reminded people that Jesus Christ was a peacemaker. He criticized the religious right's emphasis on power in *this* world. "They are confusing being a Christian soldier with being a United States soldier," he commented.

Others agree that, for all its talk about the will of God, the religious right actually puts its faith in human systems — in manmade weapons, in court-imposed censorship, in stricter laws, in religious conformity enforced by the state. It seems to them that the Moral

Majority, Christian Voice, and similar groups are more concerned with earthly power than with spiritual matters.

Billy Graham is one born-again Christian with serious doubts about the religious right. Graham is a missionary and perhaps the best-known evangelist in the world. But he sees danger in the religious right's stress on preparation for war. He is troubled by its lack of interest in such problems as world hunger. "How can we be indifferent to the millions and millions who live on the brink of starvation each year, while the nations of the world spend $550 billion each year on weapons?" Graham asked an audience of religious broadcasters in 1981. Graham also speaks out against the religious right's pride in its accomplishments, including its accomplishments in the 1980 election, its grasping for political power, and its emphasis on money. Although Graham believes Americans should hold to the tradition of applying their religious convictions to public life, he questions the specific goals and tactics of some members of the religious right.

Another who questions what the religious right is doing is Jim Wallis. Wallis is the editor of *Sojourners*, an evangelical magazine with a liberal social and political point of view. He is distressed by what he sees as the religious right's selfishness. "The evangelical movement," Wallis says, "is presented in terms of what Jesus can do for me."

Criticism of another position of the religious right, its insistence that "the Bible is God's rule book," comes from Dr. Rockne McCarthy. McCarthy is head of the Association for Public Justice, which studies politics and society from a Christian standpoint. He believes that the Bible should be used neither as a political science or biology textbook nor as a marriage manual. Its ancient stories, poems, proverbs, commandments, and prophecies, however wise and beautiful, cannot be used as literal prescriptions for national programs and international relations in the twentieth century. Instead, McCarthy believes, "God has told us what the great commandments are and we must work out [their] implications."

Work out is the key phrase. Our society has changed and we do face problems, serious problems for which we must find solutions. The rigid, theocratic solutions of the religious right, however, cannot fit into the structure of our democracy. The solutions need to come from all of us, working together under the Constitution.

10. Church, State, and the Future

Separation of church and state — what does it mean in American life?

Three hundred fifty years ago, there was one place in the Western Hemisphere where religious dissenters were not persecuted by the authorities of the state. In Rhode Island, Roger Williams's lively experiment protected men and women of all faiths.

In 1789, the lively experiment was written into the United States Constitution. The adoption of Article VI and the First Amendment liberated the federal government from the rigid dogmas of the former colonies. It made that government the government of all Americans. Freed of religious squabbling and strife, the federal government could concentrate on unifying and building the new nation. America flourished.

Separation also enabled America's religions to thrive. Since no sect was officially persecuted, nor any favored above all others, each had the chance to seek converts and grow strong. At first, most sects were Protestant. But as time passed members of other religious groups began flooding into the country. Each group had its own particular contribution to make to American life and culture. Because church and state were separate, each contribution could eventually make itself felt in public life.

Through the years, separation continued to serve the country well. Churches grew strong, but none came to dominate the country politically. The wall of separation stood firm.

Yet churches have influenced American government and politics. The abolitionist movement arose partly out of the Second Awakening of the early nineteenth century. Laws that protect the rights of workers, including child-labor laws, owe a great deal to pressure from religious groups. So do social service programs, slum clearance projects, educational programs, and the improved treatment of criminals and the insane. Today, the civil rights movement still draws much of its leadership from among the clergy.

What of tomorrow? What will separation mean in the future?

It will certainly mean continued arguments over the precise meaning of the First Amendment. Accommodationists will still say that the free-exercise clause means government ought to be doing more to help church-run schools, hospitals, and the like. Separationists will reply that the antiestablishment clause compels government to maintain a strictly hands-off attitude toward religious institutions. Arguments over school prayer, an antiabortion amendment, and government attempts to regulate religion will go on, too.

Separation also means that Americans in and out of government will continue to act publicly on their own moral and religious convictions. From our cathedrals and temples, from our synagogues and meetinghouses, will come many of the suggestions for coping with national and international problems: the nuclear arms race, energy shortages, hunger here and abroad, social injustice, greed, and corruption. Out of our houses of worship will come much of the will to face such problems — and much of the inspiration to solve them.

For our Constitution and our Bill of Rights do not forbid us to bring our religious beliefs to bear upon affairs of state. America's lively experiment means a system of government that can take advantage of the best in each faith and creed.

For Further Reading

Horowitz, Irving Louis, ed. *Science, Sin, and Scholarship: The Politics of Reverend Moon and the Unification Church.* Cambridge, Mass.: The MIT Press, 1978.

Morgan, Richard E. *The Supreme Court and Religion.* New York: The Free Press, 1972.

Morgan, Richard E. *The Politics of Religious Conflict.* Washington, D.C.: University Press of America, 1980.

Pfeffer, Leo. *Church, State, and Freedom.* Boston: The Beacon Press, 1953.

Polishook, Irwin H. *Roger Williams, John Cotton and Religious Freedom: A Controversy in New and Old England.* Englewood Cliffs, N.J.: Prentice-Hall, 1967.

Stokes, Anson Phelps, and Pfeffer, Leo. *Church and State in the United States.* New York: Harper & Row, 1950, 1964.

Index